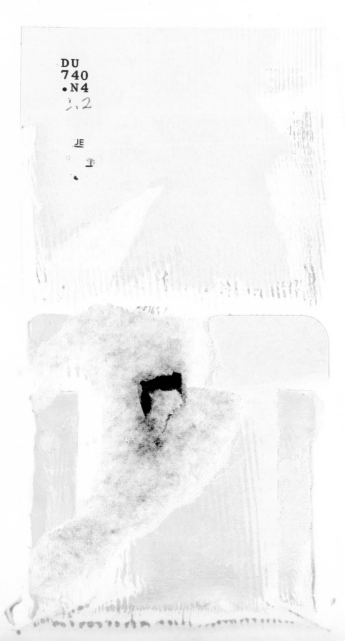

CASE STUDIES IN

CULTURAL ANTHROPOLOGY

GENERAL EDITORS

George and Louise Spindler

STANFORD UNIVERSITY

Knowing the Gururumba

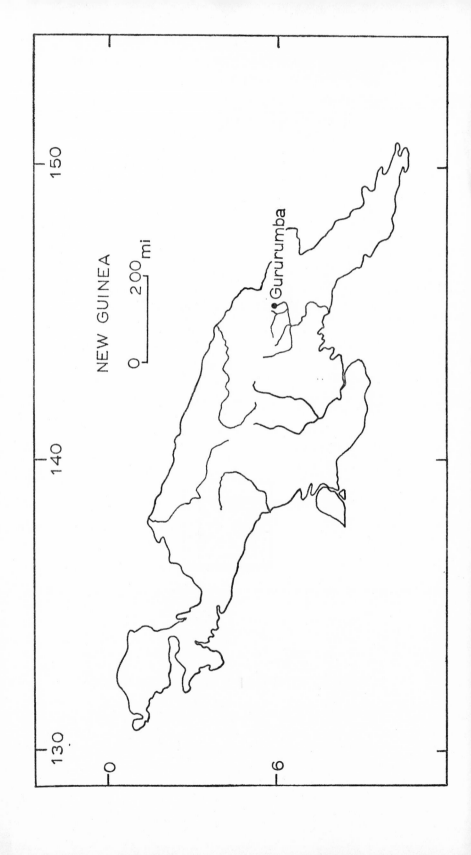

NEW GUINEA

Gururumba

0 ____ 200 mi

KNOWING THE GURURUMBA

BY

PHILIP L. NEWMAN

University of California
at
Los Angeles

HOLT, RINEHART AND WINSTON

NEW YORK   CHICAGO   SAN FRANCISCO   TORONTO   LONDON

Foreword

About the Series

These case studies in cultural anthropology are designed to bring to students in the social sciences insights into the richness and complexity of human life as it is lived in different ways and in different places. They are written by men and women who have lived in the societies they write about, and who are professionally trained as observers and interpreters of human behavior. The authors are also teachers, and in writing their books they have kept the students who will read them foremost in their minds. It is our belief that when an understanding of ways of life very different from one's own is gained, abstractions and generalizations about social structure, cultural values, subsistence techniques, and other universal categories of human social behavior become meaningful.

About the Author

Philip L. Newman is now an assistant professor at the University of California, Los Angeles. His graduate training in Anthropology was received at the University of Washington from 1955 to 1959. The field study reported on here was undertaken in 1959 and 1960 under grants from the Fulbright Commission and the Bollingen Foundation. The field materials were written up as a doctoral dissertation while he was an Ogden Mills Fellow at the American Museum of Natural History in New York, the Ph.D. being awarded in 1962. He has also carried out less extended periods of field work among the Aleut, the Nootka, and the Skokomish.

About the Book

The Gururumba live in six large villages in the upper Asaro Valley, New Guinea, at about 5500 feet elevation, bounded by towering mountains, some rising to 15,000 feet. They are a fascinating people, only very recently in contact with Western culture.

The author tells us not only about the pattern of Gururumba life, but also of the way the ethnographer discovers what the patterns are, and how he sorts them into analytic categories and forms connections among them. We see the Gururumba in their natural setting, and then how their behavior is patterned and arranged in social groups and roles. But the treatment goes beyond the analysis of social structure to give us a dramatic picture of the values and meaning of life.

The author gives us a most unusual analysis of the symbolic value of specific behaviors in ritual situations. So we come to an understanding of why the sounding of the flutes at the pig festival makes the Gururumba feel that others hearing them will "know we are strong and wonder at us"; why a girl reaching sexual maturity crawls through a sugar cane hoop to make her attractive to suitors; why men purify themselves by pushing small bundles of sharp-edged grass in and out of their nostrils to make their noses bleed; how eating half-decayed flesh symbolizes the presocial era of human life as the Gururumba conceptualize it.

Not content to leave us with only the rules for behavior in this culture, the author ends with episodes from his observations of specific persons to show how one knows the Gururumba individually and sees them operating within the cultural patterns described. He shows how this culture creates certain strains and does not resolve them, and how individuals are never simple replicas of cultural norms in their personal behavior.

George and Louise Spindler
General Editors

Stanford, California
December 1964

Contents

Foreword   vii

Introduction   1

1. The People, The Setting, The Beginning   5
   Preparing the Way, 5
   Arriving on the Scene, 8
   Settling in, 11
   Discovering the "Look" of Things, 13

2. The Strategy of Counting   16
   The Lay of the Land, 16
   People on the Land, 18
   Counting Kin, 24

3. Focusing on Groups   27
   Identifying Groups, 27
   Who Are the Gururumba? 30
   The Larger Picture, 33
   The Smaller Picture, 34
   Other Kinds of Groups, 37

4. Focusing on Roles   39
   Men and Women, 40
   Leaders, 43
   Curers, 44
   Kinsmen, 46

5. The Flow of Objects   51
   Gift Exchange in the Gururumba Setting, 51
   Gift Exchange and the Ordering of Daily Affairs, 54
   Gift Exchange and Gururumba Society, 58

6. Ritual and Social Structure   62
   Nature Spirits and the Family, 62
   Rituals of the Lineage, 64
   The Ward and the Men's Cult, 66
   The Sib and the Pig Festival, 68

The Phratry and the jaBirisi *Ceremony, 70*
Groups and Rituals, 71

7. A Theme in Supernaturalism   72
    The Concern with Growth and Strength, 72
    Growth and Strength: Productivity and Assertiveness, 74
    Productivity, Assertiveness, and Sexual Energy, 76
    Male and Female Sexuality, 79
    Body and Cosmos, 81

8. A View of Man and Society   83
    The Realm of Lusu, *83*
    System in the Realm of Lusu, *88*
    Of Pigs and Men, 92

9. Patterns and People   94
    Gambiri, 94
    Tomu, 97
    Namo, 98
    Sekau, 100
    LEnduwe, 102
    DaBore, 104

Glossary   107

Recommended Reading   109

Preparing a food offering for a domesticated nature spirit. The dome-shaped structure in front of the miniature earth oven is the spirit house.

Filling an earth oven with water from bamboo tubes.

Villagers from Miruma arriving as mourners at a funeral in another village.

A newly planted sweet potato garden. Branches have been removed from the trees in the garden to reduce shade.

Men carrying away gifts from a food distribution. The man in the foreground is carrying peanuts, a crop introduced by Australians.

The entrance to the village of Miruma. The men's house is in the foreground.

Knowing the Gururumba

Introduction

ALL OF US at some time or another have been in the position of a stranger, not knowing what actions others expected of us nor what actions we could expect of others. However, the degree of strangeness in a situation can vary a great deal. A man brought up in Los Angeles who moves to New York city will find most of his expectations about people's behavior fulfilled. With only minor adjustments he will be able to operate in the new situation and interact with the people there. If, however, he moves into a community of forest-dwelling people in the Amazon basin, he will find his habitual system of expectations so unreliable that unless the host community has special techniques designed to care for strangers, he may not survive. Such differences, whether small or large scale, are cultural differences, and their description and explanation is an important part of the anthropological enterprise. The anthropologist interested in analyzing a culture other than his own is a stranger; his first task, therefore, is to learn the expectations and understandings the members of that alien group assume as a basis for interacting. He is a special kind of a stranger, however, because he attempts to be as conscious as possible of the way he gains this knowledge, and because he must make it explicit and formulate it in categories that will allow comparison with what is discovered about other cultures. While a stranger who is not an anthropologist may gain knowledge of an alien culture sufficient to operate effectively in it, he is not likely to know how he gained it or be able to reproduce it systematically.

The task of systematically discovering and describing cultural difference is called ethnography, and the task of analyzing it with reference to some limited problem is called ethnology. Each task complements the other, and understanding the process of coming to know another culture is as important as understanding what comes to be known about it. This is the case because the ethnologist's methods of analysis, theoretical commitment, choice of problem, and even his personality affect the range of facts he will attend and his understanding of them.

The range of data-gathering techniques, substantive foci, and methods of analysis available to the ethnologist is a respectably wide one. The techniques stress procedures that put him in intimate contact with the people he is studying, much like the stranger who discovers the properties of an alien situation by operating in it. Within this procedural limit, however, individual ethnographers mix participation in the daily affairs of the group with informal conversation, structured interviews, systematic observation, administration of tests, and the noting of events as they happen, in varying proportions. The selection of substantive foci also varies, for if the problem chosen requires a broad knowledge of many facets of the culture an attempt will be made to provide approximately equal coverage of a number of categories while in another problem coverage may be restricted to one or a few categories. Such categories as technology, economics, individual life cycle, religion, kinship, politics, and art, are frequently used, but these do not form a systematically interrelated set; others can be used as effectively. The concepts available to analyze data brought together in these categories include culture area, social structure, social function, ethos, basic personality, and ecology, among others. Each analytical concept cuts across the categories using data from all or postulating relationships among them. Each also implies a theory about the events, forms, or systems defined by the categories.

Each of the above techniques and concepts produces data of a distinctive kind and views it in a distinctive way. It is therefore important in assessing what an ethnologist communicates about a culture to understand the techniques and methods he uses to gather the data as well as to understand the results of their use. This case study is concerned with learning about a human group in both these senses. It will reveal something about the patterns of an alien culture and something about the process of discovering those patterns.

Implied, therefore, is that this case study begins with the life history of the author, for if the results of ethnography are in part the product of the investigator's personality, then his findings cannot be judged accurately unless his personality is known. Indeed, there was a period when it was suggested that ethnographers be psychoanalyzed before undertaking field work to use knowledge about the limitations and biases arising from the investigator's personality as a corrective. Not many took this extreme suggestion, preferring to rely on the objectivity built into their descriptive techniques and analytic constructs, and the self-awareness inculcated through training. It cannot be denied, however, that the way an ethnographer reacts to a new cultural setting and the behavior he is observing, what he experiences as deprivation and how he handles this experience, his awareness of how others are reacting to him, the kind of role he adopts, and many other responses derive in large part from his personality. These factors not only affect the way the people he is observing act in his presence, but also influence his very perception of what they are doing. Some of these problems will be discussed in various parts of the text, but my main concern will be with the techniques and concepts used to observe and describe an alien culture rather than with what is sometimes called "the personal equation."

The choice of New Guinea as an area of study was in part made on a subjective basis. During both undergraduate and graduate study, I had been fascinated by the published accounts of New Guinea peoples to the point of naïve romanticism. Fortunately New Guinea, especially the highland area, was an important area ethnographically. Its people had not experienced extensive contact with Westerners, and there were few reports on the cultures existing there. Not only could useful descriptive work be done, but the existing accounts indicated these cultures might be especially suitable for the investigation of a particular problem: the way individuals use, manipulate, and experience their religion. This was focused on the kind of intracultural variability one can find in a small-scale, relatively homogeneous society. The published accounts indicated that the people had a rich ceremonial life but not a society overly complicated by internal differentiation of a political or economic kind. They also appeared to value "individualism," and this combined with the fact that they lived in small groups easily managed by a single worker made them seem suitable for investigation of the problem.

Selecting the Gururumba as the particular group for study accommodated both research and personal needs. I learned from another anthropologist who had worked there that the upper Asaro valley, where the Gururumba live, contained peoples who had not yet been studied but who adjoined culturally different peoples on four sides who had been studied. Knowledge about the Gururumba would thus contribute to the accumulating information concerning the regional variability of highland groups. The degree of contact with Western culture in the upper Asaro valley had apparently not produced massive change but was extensive enough so that the groups no longer practiced warfare and some of the young men knew how to speak Neo-Melanesian, a pidgin language that could be used as a mode of communication. I also learned there was a road into the upper Asaro valley from the Australian governmental center of Goroka some twenty miles away and that an Australian coffee planter as well as a missionary were not far away. These facts were important since my wife and two small children were accompanying me. They meant that medical aid and food supplies would be available without excessive delay or complication, and that our safety would be reasonably certain. In New Guinea these are not inconsequential considerations. Of the several tribes living in the valley the Gururumba were chosen because they were near the end of the road and centrally located with respect to other groups.

These particular details should not be taken as representative of those considered by all ethnologists deciding on a field site. For some the decision is more closely related to considerations of problem, which may involve a particular constellation of variables found only in a severely limited number of cases and so dictate their choice of site. Others may specialize in a given area but work there on a variety of problems. Or the choice may be less systematic when circumstances bring some to a place that suggests certain lines of investigation. Several of the classic monographs in anthropology have come about in just this way. What should be clear, however, is that the ethnologist's basic research tool in the field is himself. Consequently what he does, how he does it, and even where he does it is partially a product of the kind of person he is as well as the kind of problem he has in mind. The actual field situation rather than the carefully constructed laboratory situation is still the primary source of the ethnologist's data, and the main recording instrument is still the human observer rather than the machine. Observation, therefore, is affected by many kinds of factors extraneous to the act of observation because ethnology is a science that has not yet separated the instrument of observation from the instrument of analysis.

The People, The Setting, The Beginning

"How long will you stay, red man?"

Preparing the Way

A TRAINED ETHNOLOGIST is not a stranger to an alien culture in the same way a non-ethnologist is. His background includes extensive reading in the accumulated literature on cultures of many types and from many areas of the world. This literature begins with the earliest records and although not all of equal quality, it provides enough knowledge about the variability of culture so that we no longer expect to find human groups whose general way of life falls outside the reported range. Ethnography still reveals cultural differences, and will continue to reveal them, but the magnitude of these discovered differences is not as great as it once was, at least with respect to the cultural features ethnologists habitually consider. In fact, enough is known so that if an ethnologist hears of a newly discovered group characterized by horticulture, root crops, stone tools, and an upland environment, his knowledge of the range of human culture will allow him to make accurate judgments about several other aspects of the culture of the group as well.

In addition to this general background the ethnologist attempts to prepare himself for the specific area he plans to work in by reading whatever material is already available on it or similar areas. There are several general reasons for this. First, it will probably be the case that the people he wants to investigate speak a language he does not know. Since language is the first key to understanding another culture he must learn it. If he can gain some command of the language from published accounts before going to the field it will save him a great deal of time once he gets there. If there are no published accounts he may have to learn a related language or a pidgin language which can be used with an interpreter until he masters the local language in the field. In some cases neither can be done in advance and he must rely on his ability and training to learn the language on the spot. Second, some research problems require prior knowledge of an area because they are focused on certain variables or phenomena having a limited areal distribution. Third, the ethnologist, if possible, wants to be cognizant of behaviors that may be expected of him as a newcomer to a group or of attitudes the people hold toward members of his race. If he can know these things in advance he can adjust his behavior accordingly and reduce the possibility of creating tensions during the initial period of his stay. He will inevitably make mistakes and create tensions anyhow, but minimizing them initially will help create attitudes toward him conducive to achieving a solution. Finally, many practical matters need to be planned. Some knowledge of the climate, health problems, modes of transportation, type of available shelter, availability of food, and the like, can usually be obtained in advance. This helps the ethnologist plan for various exigencies of self-maintenance, without which the field project might fail.

Fortunately for us, some important information was available on the peoples in the upper Asaro valley: They spoke a language closely related to that spoken in the lower Asaro valley, and they were in close contact with peoples in the Chimbu valley to the west who spoke quite a different language. Neither of these languages had been analyzed in the published literature so it was impossible to learn them in advance. Effective control by the Australian government had been established in the area for about ten years, and some of the younger men who had worked for the government or as laborers under a government-controlled labor program could speak Neo-Melanesian, a pidgin language utilizing a mixed vocabulary from European and Melanesian languages but with its distinctive syntax. I learned the rudiments of this language in advance from published sources and used it to establish communication immediately in the field.

From knowledge about highland New Guinea peoples in general, I could expect that those in the upper Asaro valley would live in villages rather than scattered homesteads, would be horticulturalists raising several varieties of sweet potato as their staple crop and keeping pigs, dogs, and chickens as domesticated animals, and their physical environment would be mountainous, cool, and damp. The technology would feature gardening techniques based on a system of rotating plots rather than soil replenishment through fertilization, watering by rainfall rather than irrigation, and the use of simple hand tools rather than animal drawn implements. Items such as digging sticks, axes, knives, arrows, or spears would be made of wood and ground stone, except as metal objects of European origin had replaced them, and there would be some pottery of a simple type imported from other groups. Social organization would reveal broadly defined units, such as dialect groups, divided into relatively small, politically autonomous territorial units and further divided into smaller groupings based on some combination of organizational principles centering around kinship and identification with a locality. The division of labor would be simple, based primarily on age and sex, and leadership would derive from personal qualities rather than from occupancy of a titled position.

There was no published information on the upper Asaro peoples specifically but there were accounts of the closely related Gahuku-Gama and Siane to the south and the southwest, and the more distantly related Chimbu and Gende to the west and northeast. Certain cultural similarities were discernable among these groups, making it probable that they would also be found in the upper Asaro valley. For example, such patterns as patrilineal descent, patrivirilocal residence, bride price, polygyny, ceremonialized economic exchange, and the men's club house were found throughout the area.[1] Belief in ghosts, demonic nature spirits, witches, and sorcerers also appeared to be prevalent. Some idea of the "character" of the people could also be found in the published materials as various authors noted that they were "flamboyant," "forceful," "materialistic," or that the culture was "male dominated."

Something was learned of the living conditions from conversations with other people who had been in the general vicinity. The area was said to be relatively healthy for persons coming from the United States. Unlike the hot humid coastal areas of New Guinea, the highlands are cool and fresh, and respiratory infections or dysentery would be more serious health problems than malaria or fungus infestations. We would be able to provide ourselves with vegetables from the native peoples, but would have to rely on tinned goods for meat and most fruits. We would probably be greeted with a mixture of curiosity and suspicion, since racially and culturally we were still something of a novelty and our motives would be difficult to comprehend, but hostility was not expected.

All these items of information, and others as well, served to build up a set of expectations concerning the nature of the cultural patterns we would find and what it would be like to live in that situation for a year. It might seem that if an ethnologist were attempting to be objective about his research, these expectations would hamper him and measures should be taken to limit their prior formation. In order to understand why this is not as harmful as it might seem, think again about the ethnologist and the untrained stranger. When the stranger encounters an alien group he attempts to operate in the new situation by identifying, connecting, and explaining events produced by an unknown culture pattern in terms of the classificatory schemes and explanatory principles of his own culture. If the magnitude of cultural difference is great he will find this a largely inadequate procedure producing behavioral "mistakes" because he cannot properly identify what kind of action he is viewing, does not know what actions properly follow one another, and cannot explain why the sequences of actions he does see should follow one another. His knowledge of culture patterns in the new setting will be distorted because he tries to make the behaviors he observes meaningful in terms of culture patterns from which they did not derive. The ethnologist, on the other hand, knows that much of his foreknowledge will be inadequate or even erroneous, but having this knowledge provides a series of reference points designed for cross-

[1] See Glossary for explanation of technical terms.

cultural use and hence less subject to distortion than those provided by his own nonanthropological culture. He does not expect what he sees to be meaningful in terms of the culture patterns useful at home in everyday affairs, but expects to use another set of patterns, constituting part of the culture of anthropology, to order what he sees so that meaning will be discovered. For example, to know that the people in the upper Asaro valley reckon descent patrilineally is also to know that they do not classify kinsmen in the same way contemporary Americans do. Furthermore, to use the language of our own system of kin terms could not possibly uncover the principles involved in their system of classification. The ethnologist in this situation knows he must begin by describing the designata of alien terms in a language calculated to be culturally neutral.

Arriving on the Scene

Only so much can be done in advance and the day arrives when the ethnologist must inject himself into the situation he wishes to study and begin discovering just what makes him a stranger to a particular group. As might be imagined the experience is not an easy one, and as my family and I traveled up the road toward the head of the Asaro valley in a rented Land Rover laden with supplies we wondered how the explanation of our presence and purpose would be received, how we would locate the appropriate person to explain ourselves to, what kind of impression we would create, and many other things. We knew there would be shelter available, for our destination was the government rest house near the native village of Miruma. Rest houses, usually made of poles and thatch, are established at central locations throughout the highlands where patrol officers can stay in the course of traveling about on affairs of native administration. It would be available to us until such time as we could construct our own house.

We turned off the main road and bumped along the ridge top leading to Miruma. As we neared the rest house people began swarming around our vehicle until it was halted by the impenetrability of their mass. We had expected a few people to greet us because our progress up the valley had been shouted far ahead as we passed by villages and gardens located near the road, but not the three or four hundred there. This gathering was not primarily due to our coming, however, but a result of two other events. We became aware of the first as an Australian official came out of the rest house and introduced himself as a government doctor on medical patrol. He had been at Miruma for several days performing various minor therapeutic tasks and gathering data on the health of the natives. Many were there because the doctor had called them in from surrounding villages for medical examination; others were there voluntarily, seeking relief from their ailments.

Thus it was that the first person we explained ourselves to was the doctor. The doctor, in turn, called in the *luluai* and *tultul* from the native village situated along the ridge directly behind the rest house. *Luluais* and *tultuls* are government-appointed native officials. The *luluai* is responsible for maintaining order in the community under his jurisdiction, carrying out any directives given him by the government, bringing matters of dispute that cannot be settled in the community before a patrol officer or district commissioner, and keeping possession of the village book. This book, kept current by patrol officers, contains census information, a record of patrols into the area, and notes concerning local incidents relevant to the administration of justice. The *tultul,* in theory, is a kind of assistant to the *luluai.* Both men arrived quickly, and after pushing their way through the surrounding crowd, stood before us at attention giving both my wife and myself the hand salute accorded government officials. The doctor took some pains to explain, through an interpreter, that we were neither government officials nor missionaries, but that we were in the area to learn the people's "fashion." He charged the *luluai* with looking after our welfare and seeing that our needs were met. After another salute the two men left and shouted their newly gained information to the people gathered around us as they proceeded back to the village. The doctor, assuring us that everything would now be taken care of, went back to giving innoculations and pulling teeth, and we moved our supplies into one of the small huts near the rest house designed to accommodate the contingent of native police that accompany most patrols.

We spent the next few hours establishing ourselves in the hut that was to be our home until the medical patrol left, while the native people gave us an initial scrutiny. In some instances the examination clearly put us in the category of objects. Older people, especially women, felt our bodies, pinched our flesh, and fingered our hair. One man, apparently sensing a golden opportunity to relieve a long-standing curiosity about footgear, removed my boots and socks so he could examine them, and my feet, in detail. Some young boys concentrated on imitating my stride and elements of my stance and posture. In other instances our objects rather than ourselves were the point of curiosity. Cameras, watches, mirrors, air mattresses, stoves, pans, items of clothing were familiar to them, but they discovered we put few restrictions on their handling and examining these things—a practice not followed by most nonnatives they had encountered. It led almost immediately to unexpected results, some of which we were aware of and some not. We were aware that people began demanding we relinquish various items that caught their fancy, not by sale, barter, or gift exchange, but uncommitted transfer. It became irritating, and we soon had to give up our pretense of openness in order to retain our possessions. It was some time before we understood some of the reasons for their behavior and I am not sure they ever understood the reasons for ours. For one thing, it was incomprehensible that two adults and two children could need, consume, or own the large amount of "stuff" we unloaded. Not being able to discern any reasonable need on our part for all these things, the freedom of access allowed to them was taken by some as an invitation to claim whatever they wanted. We were not aware, however, of more subtle attempts to claim part of this unprecedented bounty. Small bundles of native-grown food were presented to us or simply left at our doorstep. If the giver appeared in person, he would say that no "pay" or "return" was expected since the *luluai* had instructed everyone to bring us food. We accepted them naively, not suspecting that with each presentation the giver publicly announced to his fellows he was thereby claiming the right to enter into future negotiations with us for some specific item in our possession. Days, and even weeks, after arriving I would occasionally be put in the position of making someone angry because I would not enter into negotiations for the immediate transfer of my coat, my wife's hat, or some other item claimed on that first day.

It was somewhat puzzling that except for the brief meeting with the *luluai* and *tultul* arranged by the doctor no one had appeared to ask questions concerning our presence, so after the Land Rover had been emptied and started back down the road I walked into the village of Miruma. It was crowded and, judging from the piles of food and the arrangement of people, it seemed obvious an event of some public importance was in progress. This, then, was the second reason for the large number of people we encountered. My entry caused no stir whatsoever and several attempts to elicit the reason for the gathering only produced the answer that it was "nothing." Someone finally said it was a betrothal, which prompted me to begin taking notes, but nothing was recorded except what could be seen because most questions about the details of what I saw were answered by saying I was seeing "nothing."

As the afternoon passed, it became increasingly difficult to see any pattern in the response being given us. On the one hand we were the objects of intense curiosity and on the other we were being politely ignored. It was only in the evening, after the guests at the betrothal left the village, that I began to understand what was happening. At that time I returned to the village and sat down in front of the door to the men's house. The men inside stopped their conversation to inquire what I wanted, and when they found I wanted to come in were quite pleased to steer me through the low doorway and arrange a place for me in the crowded dwelling. Not knowing exactly what to say or do after getting inside, I resorted to the time-consuming process of lighting my pipe while waiting for them to question me. The lulai asked, "How long will you stay, red man?" I answered "a year" and added that my family would remain with me. This precipitated a long discussion punctuated by expressions of surprise between the older men and the young man who had been translating in Neo-Melanesian. It developed that although Neo-Melanesian counts time by "moons" there was no corresponding system of time-reckoning in the native language making it difficult to effect a translation. More important, it had not previously occurred to anyone that we were intending to stay for an extended period of time as a family unit. Nonnatives who were neither government officials nor missionaries had come to the village before, but had not stayed for long periods, contenting themselves with walking in the forest for a few days collecting plants and animals or with watching a single, short ceremony. Our arrival on the day of a betrothal put us in this latter class, and it had been assumed that if we did not leave with the doctor we would soon after. No one bothered about our presence because it had been perceived as inconsequential except for curiosity value or the prospect of gaining access to our supplies. In other words, after a day in the community we had not yet arrived.

What happened that first day in Miruma is an example of the difficulties the ethnologist can encounter in attempting to connect himself meaningfully to an alien community. In this case it could be said the difficulty was of communication, that because of preoccupation with the betrothal ceremony no one took the time fully to attend the implications of the information they received about us. However, since that first day's experience was repeated, it cannot be fully explained by the occasion. It can be partially explained as the difficulty in bringing people to comprehend a totally unfamiliar social role for which their culture provides few analogies. There was no precedent in this culture for a person whose only purpose in a community was to examine its "fashion." It is true that native people sometimes went to alien places specifically to observe dances or rituals different from their own, and that they received both natives and nonnatives into their community for the same reason. But such occasions were of short span and focused observation on a limited range of activity. Furthermore, prior to the cessation of warfare under Australian control, such journeys by natives were limited to those communities with which a person had already established other kinds of ties and purposes so that his activity as an observer of alien ways was part of a larger action context. When the people gathered in the men's house learned our stay would be long, they began to realize I was a different kind of person than they had yet encountered and, although they never fully understood my purposes, the process of taking me into account had begun.

Settling In

During the next ten days no attempt was made to carry out my systematic ethnography. The time was given over to establishing a household and to building a basis for interaction with the community. The latter task is not one the ethnographer can execute according to a plan as easily as he can the former because its form and impetus must come partly from the community itself. Since this is the case, the form it takes is itself indicative of the culture patterns the ethnologist is attempting to discover.

Both the form and the impetus came with unexpected formality and dispatch on the second day. I had planned to have a house built near the village of Miruma because it was convenient both to water and the road, appeared to be centrally located with respect to several native villages, and had a commanding view of the Asaro valley. The announcement of this plan was anticipated by a delegation of men from Miruma headed by the *luluai* and *tultul* who came before me and proclaimed that henceforth I was to be considered by all as "their red man." They pointed out that another group living down-river "had a red man," a coffee planter, and that a second group living up-river had one, a missionary. They further suggested that although they too occasionally possessed such a person when the rest house was occupied, it would be highly desirable to have a permanent resident. I had only to indicate my choice of plot and a house would be built. My "acceptance" of their "offer," if one can apply those terms to what was essentially acquiescence to a demand, involved much more than anticipated, but for that reason established the first important link connecting me to life of the village.

The link was primarily an economic one calculated to produce both direct and indirect gains. They counted on selling me the ground on which to build a house and were already figuring the price of construction. They supposed I would hire people to work in the house after the manner of other red men they knew. It was reasoned that all red men had a "business," and although mine was not altogether clear, it was certain to mean income. (Despite efforts to explain myself on the previous day, consensus was that I would open a trade store featuring very low prices.) The indirect benefits, if not precisely formulated, were grand in scope. At that time and place in highlands New Guinea it was prestigeful to "have a red man." The reasons for this are complex, but they are involved with the native attitude that the presence of a red man presages an improvement in the general state of affairs, especially an increase in the ability to control wealth and material things. I did not fully understand it at the time, but this was what people were expressing when they came up after it became known we would settle in Miruma and made such statements as, "It is all right now." "Everything will occur now." "The past is finished." Or, "You have come, now everyone (other native groups) will eat our pigs." The last statement hopefully connected our coming with increased prestige of the community through exchange activity traditionally accompanied by the eating of cooked pork. The outcome of such exchange activities is calculated in terms of gains in prestige, but already established prestige is a factor in achieving a gain. In other words, to be known as a person from the village where a red man dwells is to have an advantage over persons from other villages because of the potential wealth and power he represents.

Having a red man in your midst can be a disillusioning experience, however. Natives living in the lower Asaro valley where red men are relatively plentiful no longer have high expectations of great material benefit flowing from their presence. Given the fact that the people of Miruma have frequent contact with these groups, the fact that some of the young men had worked for red men in Goroka and other places, and the fact that both the missionary and the planter were close at hand, raises the question of why they maintained these expectations. Subsequent investigation revealed they did not maintain them at a very high level, but my coming had increased the level considerably. The reason was simple. In efforts to explain myself, I had used the device of contrast, of stressing the differences between myself and the other kinds of red men they knew. The effect of this was not an understanding of what it meant to live with a people in order to study their "fashion," but only the understanding that I was different from other red men. In their minds, the stress placed on differences indicated I was the red man they hoped for rather than the red man they knew.

One other factor enters into this situation—the mystic quality of red men. In the initial contact between Australians and natives of this area, the Australians were frequently perceived as ghosts. It did not take the natives long to discover they were not ghosts, but some of the attitudes held toward ghosts still carry over to these intruders on the native scene. The native term for them, "red men," indicates the existence of these attitudes, for ghosts are thought to be red. Various authors writing on these attitudes and their effects in other areas of New Guinea point out that one of the most persistently puzzling things about red men is their ability to generate and control vast amounts of material goods. Since production processes are not seen by native peoples, red man's ability to command resources derives from an unknown basis. It is, for many, a mystic process controlled by mystic means producing miraculous results. This helps account for the high level of expectation characteristic of links established with red men and the fact that the people of Miruma expected both very specific and very general benefits to flow from my presence.

At the time of arrival in Miruma I was not aware of the extent to which these factors were operative or, in some cases, that they existed. I only knew people seemed to be pleased we were there and acted in a way that fit well with my plans. Arrangements to build a house were easily made, a site for it selected, and two young men agreed to work for us as cook and gardener. The cook had worked for red men before and knew how to light a primus stove, the necessity for boiling water, and the preparation of simple meals. He therefore seemed acceptable. The gardener was an adolescent boy who, because most plant tending is done by women in his culture, did not know much about gardening at all, but seemed to know more than we did. A third young man was hired at a later date to act as guide and interpreter. All these seemingly smoothly executed acts had unforeseen consequences deriving from the people's attitude toward me as a red man. Some of them will be discussed in subsequent chapters.

Discovering the "Look" of Things

In the initial phases of field work there is a great deal going on around the ethnographer that completely eludes him. During the settling in period I was beginning to realize the importance attached to economic affairs simply from the number of times such affairs came up, but only in a very limited way. For the most part, the idiom of social action constituting the culture of these people was unknown to me, and frequently all I "saw" when looking at people, even when they seemed to be interacting, were human figures against a natural background. There were, of course, many times when these scenes appeared meaningful, but training induced me to be cautious in attributing a meaning to them until greater access was gained through systematic observation to the idiom in which they were conducted. There was, in my case, an interesting consequence of this: a heightened awareness of differences amenable to observation in terms of physical properties.

For example, I found that everyone else was shorter than I, that roofs were not meant to be stood up under, that doorways were too small, or that the rutted foot paths and mountain side toeholds made for bare feet would not accommodate my booted foot. I could not use any of the steel-headed axes owned by natives because they had taken out the European style handles and put in round handles of small diameter tapering to a point at the end. Attempting to chop with one of these usually resulted in the implement's flying out of my hand.

Noting the way people hold and move their bodies became a kind of preoccupation. When going down hill, women habitually walk with their feet angled sharply in to prevent slipping. Men usually trot when negotiating a slope. People of the same sex may hold hands or lock arms while walking, but not people of opposite sex. Men walk in front of women. A common stance consists of arms crossed over the chest, the hands inserted in the arm pits, and one leg wound around the other. Squatting with feet flat on the ground, or sitting with legs extended fully to the front without a back rest is common. If fingers are used in counting, enumeration starts with the little finger and the ennumerated fingers are held together in a bundle rather than ticked off. Pointing is as often done with the chin as with the extended arm. Body contact is sought rather than avoided by people sitting or standing in groups. Kissing on the mouth or face is never seen between persons of any age or sex, but adults frequently kiss the genitals of infants. Greeting another person involves extensive rubbing of the arms, back, and legs, or pressing together by grasping the buttocks. Feet and toes are used in amazing conjunction with hands and fingers for a variety of tasks.

Continually stimulated awareness of differences in the physical type and dress soon began to dissolve my initial impression of sameness. All eyes remained "brown" and all hair "dark." No one's skin was darker than "dark brown," but many revealed areas of skin protected from the sun that were no darker than my own arms and legs. Faces looked "rugged" because of heavy brow ridge, prominent cheek bones, and widely flaring nostrils. Lips were "narrow" and mouths very "wide." Only old people were "thin" and only adolescent girls were "fat." Bulging abdomens were common, probably because of parasitic infestation and other disease syndromes. All these characteristics became a kind of type useful as background for identifying the variations that were individual people.

With respect to dress, people at first seemed essentially bare. This was in spite of the fact that all men and women wear some kind of pubic covering. Women wear two sets of string aprons suspended from a rope belt, a wide one in front not quite reaching the knees, and a narrow one in back reaching to the calves. Men dress in a variety of styles. Most men prefer a belt holding a free hanging length of cloth or netting in front and a bundle of leaves or grass in back. This costume is borrowed from the culturally different Chimbu living to the northwest. A few men wear the tightly fitting G-string made of bark cloth identified with Asaro valley people, and some of the young men wear shorts in the fashion of red men. Little boys go naked, but little girls never do. In addition to these larger and more obvious garments the people also cover themselves in ways that are initially less obvious. One only begins to realize the degree they detract from bareness when people are seen without them. Men commonly wear wickerwork crescents in their hair studded with small shells; a head piece of fern leaves or a knit cap; ear pendants of small shells or the bodies of irridescent green beetles; a band of small shells around the forehead; nose decorations of shell wood, or bird quills; one or more large pieces of shell around neck; a small net bag hanging under one arm; bracelets made of vines; wrist cuffs, arm bands, leg bands, and ankle cuffs made in several styles and materials. Women always have a large netted carrying bag suspended from their head, even when it is empty, that covers their back. They occasionally wear nose ornaments of wood, and frequently wear several large shells around the neck. Knit caps, arm bands, and leg bands are common for women. All women have their faces tattooed and most men have a tattoo on the back or chest. Both men and women tie large numbers of short ropes in their hair producing a "mop" effect with different styles for the two sexes. This everyday wear is replaced by more spectacular adornment, especially for men, on ceremonial occasions.

Sizes and shapes, attitudes of the body, physical type, and dress or ornamentation are only some of the more obvious areas defining the "look of things." In situations where communication is at a minimum because of language differences they become points of concentration since they are readily accessible to observation and amenable to an ordering revealing a range of variation. The primacy of these areas in exploring the dimensions of strangeness is indicated when it is remembered that the people of Miruma as well as the ethnographer made them a focus of initial curiosity.

2

The Strategy of Counting

"Put my name in your book."

C ERTAIN INITIAL observations the ethnographer assumes will yield a large amount of material on several aspects of culture and prove useful in solving a wide range of problems. These are relatively simple to make and require only limited knowledge of the culture under investigation to ascertain their reliability. They are frequently made at the beginning of a field study not only to provide necessary background information, but also because they do not interfere too directly in the lives of the people. This is part of the strategy of counting, and devices such as a map of the area, a census, and genealogies are such starting points. The classic ethnographic monograph commonly begins with chapters on physical environment or settlement pattern elaborated from information gathered by such devices. These topics appear in the first chapters of the comprehensive description of a culture probably not so much because they are logically prior as because they are amenable to quantitative statement and description in terms of objective properties. This is not to say that other topics are necessarily unsuited to such statement, only that an efficient and useful way has not yet been found to deal with all of them in that way. They also probably represent what an ethnographer comes to know first about a culture and are just a systematic step beyond discovering the "look" of things.

The Lay of the Land

A printed map taken from aerial photographs showing the Asaro river and its tributaries, and several days of tramping about the countryside provided a basic orientation to the land. The Asaro runs approximately northwest and southeast. The northern and eastern walls of the valley are formed by the Bismarck mountains, a massive range with one peak of over 15,000 feet elevation. The western wall is formed by a subsidiary range separating the Asaro and Chimbu river systems with elevations to 11,000 feet. Steep-sided ridges extend from these bounding walls into the Asaro basin cutting it into a series of V-shaped valleys near the head of the basin and broader bays further down. In the lower part of the basin the walls are at some distance from one another thus opening the basin into a broad plain. The floor of the upper basin has an elevation of approximately 5500 to 5700 feet and runs for fifteen to twenty miles before broadening out into the lower basin. The people we are concerned with live in the smaller valleys and bays of the upper basin.

The mountains are young, geologically, giving them an abrupt, bulky appearance relieved only slightly by the fine engraving of narrow, swiftly running streams pouring down their sides. Little bare rock is visible, except for occasional limestone outcroppings, and the sharp contours of the larger ridges are softened by a thick covering of vegetation. The soil is dark and friable near the basin floor, but tends to be red and hardened with clay away from the river. The bays mentioned above are defined by limestone ridges extending almost to the river and separated from one another by varying distances ranging up to four miles. In between, the hills and spurs have a gentler, more rounded form.

Passageways through this land are not waterways, for they are too swift and shallow. Indeed, the people have no knowledge of rafts, canoes, or other forms of water transportation. Rather, there are paths extending along ridge lines or plunging directly down the precipitous slopes: the switchback trail is unknown. The government road, which runs about half way into the upper basin, is a dirt track maintained by native labor recruited through the institution of the work day. On this day, which comes once a week, all people living along the road turn out to make whatever improvements are needed on it under the supervision of *luluais* and *tultuls*. More complex tasks, such as building bridges or rerouting the road, are supervised by a government officer.

Map and compass provided an orientation for me, but these organize the landscape in quite a different way than the frame of reference employed by the people who live in it. For them, mountains and ridges are not part of the geomorphology, but part of the social universe. A ridge does not have meaning as part of a more massive earth formation, but as the boundary between human groups. Trails do not run along ridges, they go to named places. Directions are not in terms of the sun or the earth's poles, but have the more limited referents of uphill, downhill, upstream, downstream, toward or away from a place. A system like this works on the basis of a large number of invariant reference points that are local in nature. These are provided by named tribal areas, villages, plots of ground, and landmarks. The importance of knowing their names and relative locations is illustrated by the fact that their learning is not left to chance. At some point in a young boy's life he is taken to a high point on the Asaro-Chimbu divide from where almost all the upper Asaro valley can be seen. The major bays and other physical features are strikingly clear from there and the total relationship of one named part to another becomes obvious. A small ceremony is held during which he is told the names of groups occupying the various parts as well as which of them harbor friends and which enemies.

Although efforts at mapping the area produced only a rather crude chart by cartographic standards, its usefulness in revealing aspects of the culture must also be counted in assessing the utility of the operation. My seemingly random wanderings and very real difficulty in comprehending directions given by natives finally led them to put me through the little ceremony called "showing the land" given to young boys. Through it, information was gathered on the system of directions characteristic of this culture, one of the regular events in the life cycle of a male, and the names of distinguishable social groups. This last bit of information was an important prelude to analyzing the bases of social grouping.

People on the Land

A map of the land showing the way people are distributed over it is an unanalyzed description of settlement pattern. Analyzing this description produces an understanding of some of the factors people take into account when they organize themselves spatially.

The village of Miruma, along with several other villages, is located in one of the larger bays on the western wall of the Asaro valley. Since most of the villages formed two named groups counting one another as friends rather than enemies, this bay was taken as a unit of analysis on the assumption that its geographical discreetness identified some kind of social entity as well. An enlarged base map of this bay was prepared and details of settlement pattern filled in.

Putting on the base map every man-made structure found within the bay revealed the following: some structures occur singly and some in clusters; the clusters have different shapes and sizes; some clusters are far from the river and some near it; some clusters have different types of structures in them than others; and some are on the backs of ridges while others are not. At the outset it was not known how many of these variations were significant or what the reasons for them were, but they served as starting points for investigation.

The difference between houses occurring singly and in clusters is related to the fact that the people of Miruma are horticulturalists keeping small domesticated animals. Most single houses are referred to as "garden houses" or "pig houses," dwellings erected within the fenced enclosure of a garden. Gardens are not always located near villages, and these houses save a person the trouble of walking back and forth between village and garden during periods of intense gardening activity. They are also the place where a man's pigs are kept most of the time. The fact that people may reside in either the village or the garden serves other ends as well; these will be discussed below.

Two types of cluster can be distinguished on the basis of their use, shape, and the presence or absence of structures that are not dwellings. One can be called a living village and the other a ceremonial center. Villages usually consist of twenty-five or thirty houses arranged lineally. The number of houses varies from as few as ten to as many as seventy, but there are special reasons for these extremes. The houses are circular in plan featuring a conical roof topped with a long, upright pole. There are no openings except the door which faces out onto a broad path running the length of the village. The house walls consist of a row of parallel stakes stuffed with dried grass held in place by long horizontal strips of tree bark. There is no division of the interior into rooms, but a low partition may separate the front half containing a hearth from the back half containing headrests used in sleeping. The linear arrangement of houses conforms to the rather narrow ridge backs where most living villages are located, but it is usually broken by one or two larger houses standing on the opposite side of the village path from the other buildings. These are men's houses. The adult males of a village live together in men's houses while each woman has her own house.

In ceremonial centers the houses are arranged in a rectangle rather than a line. At least one side of such a center is formed by a long, shedlike, noncompartmentalized structure with many hearths in it, and the remaining sides by circular houses. The long structure is used to house guests attending certain kinds of ceremonies that require their presence in the village for several days. All the buildings face the inside of the rectangle which becomes the center for activity during a ceremony. These centers also contain a fenced enclosure, not found in living villages, having religious significance. Ceremonial centers always have fewer inhabitants than villages except on ceremonial occasions when people occupying several villages band together as hosts and move into the ceremonial center. Both types of settlement are defined by a surrounding fence, and villages may be divided at several points by transverse fences.

By taking certain features of size and location as relevant characteristics two other types of villages can be distinguished. These may be called old villages and new villages. Old villages seldom contain more than twelve to fourteen houses and are located on ridges far back from the river near the edge of the forest. New villages are three to six times larger and are located on less abrupt prominences some distance from the forest or on flat land near the river. The new villages have come into being in the last ten years and reflect changes wrought by red man's law. Before the red man came warfare was common, and the flat, open grassland along the river was a dangerous place to live because it offered no natural defensive positions. People ventured into this grassland at their peril, and it was more often exploited as a battle ground than as a subsistence area. Villages were built away from the river for defensive reasons including the proximity of the forest as a refuge in case of attack. With the cessation of warfare people began to move down from their mountain perches to take advantage of the better soil at lower elevations and also because the government urged them to settle in more accessible areas. Accessibility, which made control easier, was also a matter of consolidation and so they were urged to erect larger villages. Old villages are not entirely abandoned and new villages are not always full, but the two now exist where only one existed before.

There is one village differing from all the others in the style of its buildings. These are oval or round-ended in plan rather than circular and are divided into rooms which sometimes open onto a central passageway. It is occupied by Chimbu-speaking people, and more will be said of it below.

The information gathered in the process of filling in the map produced material of important kinds. First, there was a large amount of quantitative data pertaining to the physical arrangement of people, buildings, and villages. The bay contained seven new living villages and three ceremonial villages. The exact number of old villages was uncertain because it was difficult to locate them, but nineteen had been found. A crude estimate of population size by counting houses in new villages produced the figure 1121. Figures on houses per village, distances between villages, distances and directions of garden houses from villages, number of men's houses per village, number of transverse fences per village, and the like were recorded and stored for possible future use. Three villages, including the village of Miruma, were investigated more intensively than others in that the owner and current occupants of each house were recorded. This produced an accurate but limited census.

Second, knowledge was beginning to accumulate on the way people fit into the pattern of buildings erected on the land. This might be called the social dimension of settlement pattern because it reveals those factors separating and combining people at given times and places. The form taken initially by this knowledge provides an illustration of an ethnographer's preconceptions at work and so has interest beyond its content. In the process of going from one village to another counting houses and recording positions, it frequently seemed that the villages were "empty." There was always someone there, but it would usually turn out to be a few children playing, an old person resting, or an adult passing through to somewhere else. In the late afternoon people would begin to come into a village, but more men than women appeared, and then never all the men who had a right to be there. After some time in the field it became apparent that villages were never fully occupied except when some matter of general importance occurred. The arrival of a patrol officer, a visitor from another area with affairs to discuss, marriages, funerals, court cases, planned fights, and ceremonialized food exchanges were events of an order sufficient to fill a village for a few days. I was surprised there were not more people in a village more of the time, for to me the existence of villages implied a center of group life in the sense that people do everything habitual there except what can only be done elsewhere. These villages, however, are centers of group life in the sense that people come to them mainly to do what must be done in some larger group than the family.

Adult men come into a village for three major reasons: (1) to stay in the men's house, (2) to attend public events, and (3) because their gardens are nearby. The men's house is an information center, a decision-making center, a ritual center, and a dwelling. Men who have not slept there the previous night, frequently gather at the men's house in the morning to discuss plans for the day. They meet there, away from the hearing of outsiders and the distraction of women and children, to decide on matters of importance or to perform secret rituals. Men work in the men's house preparing costumes or practicing for ceremonial occasions and sleep there when they are in progress. A man may stay in a village because the garden plot he is currently working is nearby, but since every man has more than one plot, and they are scattered, his stay is dependent on the time spent working that plot. This, incidently, partially explains the continued use of old villages, for they are located near gardens still in use. It also explains the use of ceremonial villages during periods of ritual inactivity, for the central plaza may be converted to a garden. Adult women stay less frequently in a village than men. Young, unmarried adults commonly stay in a village. Girls are largely divorced from subsistence activities from the time of puberty to betrothal and a group of them may occupy a woman's house in a village where they receive suitors in formalized, evening courting sessions. Their agemates of opposite sex stay in the men's house which becomes a kind of dormitory for them.

Another aspect of the social dimension of settlement pattern can be seen if instead of asking what generally brings people into a village, we ask what brings the particular constellation of people together that is characteristically present in any given village. This question cannot be fully answered with the data presented to this point, but enough is known to suggest what kind of data will answer it. For example, new villages are divided into segments by transverse fences, and each segment has its own men's house. The women's houses in each segment shelter the wives of men who frequent the men's house of that segment. Each segment of a new village tends to contain the same people making up the personnel of one of the old villages. Many of the adult males in a segment claim to be descended from brothers or from a common father. All this suggests that the segments of a village may be based on a rule of patrilineal descent, and that villages themselves may be larger units built upon this base. Genealogies provide some of the data necessary to answer this question.

Before any genealogies were collected it became apparent there was one factor unrelated to the calculation of kinship operating to bring certain people together in some villages. This was the factor of conservatism. As mentioned above, new villages are located in the grassland away from the forest. Attitudes about the dangers of living in the grassland, deriving from the fact that it presents the problem of exposure to enemy attack as well as from certain supernatural beliefs, made living in these villages uncongenial to some people. They preferred to stay in the old villages and did not even build a token dwelling in the new villages. This further explains the persistence of old villages and indicates that although kinship may be a factor in organizing the personnel of a village there are other factors operating as well.

The third category of material accumulated through mapping is related to the problem of subsistence patterns and land use. Gardens and vegetation zones were put on the map as well as villages and buildings, and they form the data relevant to this category. The first obvious pattern seen in this data is a change in land use correlated with elevation. This pattern can be described in terms of use-zones. The first zone extends from the valley floor to an elevation of about 6000 feet. This zone becomes progressively narrower toward the head of the Asaro valley, but in the bay under consideration it is two or three miles wide. The natural vegetation in this zone consists primarily of a tall, reedy grass known as *pitpit* in Neo-Melanesian. It grows in clumps reaching eight or ten feet in height. The stalks and leaves of this plant are used for such things as roofing material, fences, and arrow shafts. Small animals and birds abound here and are frequently hunted for food. This was formerly a no-man's-land and is only beginning to come under cultivation.

The second zone extends from 6000 to 7500 feet. It is the zone of most intensive cultivation and all the new villages fall within it. Naturally occurring vegetation has been largely supplanted in this zone by domesticated plants, although there are remnants of an old forest cover dominated by oak trees to be seen in some of the small uncultivated gullies or along the banks of streams. It does not have the open appearance of the first zone, however, because of the remnant forest and large stands of casuarina trees planted in areas not under active cultivation or around villages. Bamboo, banana, and other tall plants are also abundant. Gardens cover the area, their fences, boundary markers of colored plants, and symmetrically arranged drainage ditches imposing a regularity on the land that marks the constant presence of man.

The third zone, ranging from 7500 to 8200 feet, is transitional between the zone of intensive cultivation and the forest. Prior to the cessation of warfare this area was under more intensive cultivation than it is now, but since then many of the more steeply inclined garden sites have been abandoned in favor of sites in the second zone. As a result, much of the area is reverting to a second growth of bushy plants, young forest trees, and giant tree ferns. Gardens are still maintained here, and pigs are allowed to root in the brush, but at the higher levels some important plants, such as sugar cane and taro, will not grow. Even the hardy sweet potato does not flourish above 8000 feet. On the other hand, some food plants do better here than at lower elevations. Pandanus trees, which yield an annual crop of highly prized nuts, are such a plant, and many kinds of wild plants found only in this zone are gathered for food or other purposes. It is interesting that people seem to prefer this zone to any of the others. They will, for example, comment that the lower zones are too hot or too dangerous because proximity to the road brings with it the possibility of sorcery attack from enemies who wander freely over it. They feel that pigs prefer the food found in this zone and that children should frequent the area for their health.

The fourth zone, which can be called the forest zone for the sake of convenience, reaches to the top of the dividing range. It is a complex of plant communities superficially divisible into an upper and lower forest. The lower forest is relatively dry and dominated by tall stands of antarctic beech, while the upper forest is damp and peaty with great accumulations of moss covering the mass of lower growing vegetation. No one lives in this zone but it is exploited for its timber, birds, marsupials, and various kinds of exotic plants including orchid vines which yield a bright yellow fibre used for decorative motifs in weaving.

The second pattern seen in this data relates to the positioning and arrangement of gardens. Gardens were not measured or examined in detail at this point in the study, but some of their general characteristics were noted in the course of locating them on the map. The positioning of gardens is largely determined by ideas the people hold concerning what kinds of plants grow best in which areas. Land ownership is also important, but land does not seem to be in short supply so that any given man usually has available to him, land of all the preferred types.

The slope of the land has little to do with whether or not it is used as a garden site. Slopes of over 45° off the horizontal are occasionally used as long as there is sufficient soil to maintain the crops. Terracing is not practiced, but long poles are staked down in rows against the slope at regular intervals on the steeper sites in an effort to check soil slippage. Irrigation or a water source is no problem because rainfall exceeds 100 inches a year. Rather, it is drainage that is one of the most serious problems, and gardens are usually oriented to facilitate maximum water run-off. Small gardens, or patches in gardens, given over principally to growing taro are the exception to this. This plant thrives in moist soil and is planted at the lower edge of gardens or in gullies or other low-lying places. Sugar cane is said to grow best at lower elevations and large portions of gardens in the first and second zones are given over to its propagation. Sweet potatoes and yams are the main crops; each comes in many varieties differing noticeably in color, texture, and taste. The people have definite notions about the need to plant certain varieties in certain kinds of soil and position their gardens accordingly.

The internal arrangement of a garden is ordered by several factors. First, what we have been calling a garden is a cultivated area defined by a fence. More than one nuclear family may have plots inside this fence, and these are separated from one another by rows of decorative plants. This gives one kind of arrangement to the garden. Second, a system of crop rotation and staggered planting is followed inside a garden as well as between gardens. Inside a garden this means some parts of it will contain mature plants, some young plants, and some will be in fallow. Third, certain combinations of plants are separated from other combinations in discreet areas of the garden. For example, sugar cane and an asparaguslike plant are commonly planted together, as are yams and a kind of native bean. Finally, drainage ditches divide the whole into a series of rectangular planting beds.

Examining the factors involved in the positioning and arrangement of gardens, besides contributing to knowledge of subsistence pattern, indicates why each man has more than one garden plot. He uses different soils and ecological zones for different crops, and he has several gardens in varying states of maturity to assure him a fairly constant food supply.

Counting Kin

In societies like the Gururumba it is assumed that social relationships based on kinship will be operative in some degree at almost all levels of social organization. Kin terms will name many roles in the society and kinship will be a principle of recruitment in various kinds of social groups. The most efficient way yet devised to begin systematically collecting data that will reveal the system of kin terms, kin ties, and the use made of kinship in forming social groups is through the collection of genealogies.

In collecting genealogies the ethnographer interviews all the adults comprising some easily identifiable unit, such as a village. He asks each person to list, in birth order if possible, all his own biological offspring, all those of his parents, the offspring of his parents' siblings, and the children of all of these. He may stop at this point or continue to the limits of the informants' knowledge, attempting to get the progeny of grandparents, the siblings of grandparents, and their children. At the same time that the names of all these people are being collected, the ethnographer also asks which of them are living, where they are living, and what kin term the informant applies to each one. In some areas of the world the ethnographer will find his informants continuing beyond the questions asked and extending the genealogy to ancestors living many generations in the past or even to supernatural figures such as creator gods. In the village of Miruma, however, it was difficult for adult informants to recall the names of ancestors removed by only two generations.

Once a mass of material of this sort has been collected it can be used in a variety of ways, but one of the initial problems the ethnographer may set himself is discovering the referent of the terms he has collected. At one level of analysis this is a simple task involving the listing of types of kinsmen referred to by a given term in the genealogies. Restricting ourselves to some kinds of consanguineal kin and assuming an adult male informant, the following list can be compiled from the genealogies collected in Miruma:

ahono	Fa, FaElBr, FaFa, MoFa.
ijEno	Mo, MoMo, FaMo, FaElSi, MoElSi.
omono	MoBr.
noho	SiCh, FaSiCh, MoBrCh.
uBono	ElBr, FaYrBr, FaElBrSon, MoElSiSo.
naku'nE	YrBr, FaYrBrSo, MoYrSiSo, ElBrSo.
atEno	ElSi, FaYrSi, FaElBrDa, MoYrSi, MoElSiDa.
aru'nE	YrSi, FaYrBrDa, MoYrSiDa.
gipE'nE	So, FaBrSoSo, MoSiSoSo.
arunE	Da, FaBrSoDa, BrDa, MoSiDaDa.
gwo'mo	FaSiChCh, MoBrChCh, SiChCh.
na'BO	SoSo, DaDa.

This simple listing is not, in itself, very informative but there are several ways in which a more generalized statement can be made concerning the referents of these terms. They can, for example, be considered in terms of contrastive groups. Consider first the three terms *ahono, iJEno,* and *omono.* In contrast to all other terms they indicate only kinsmen of senior generation to ego. *Ahono* and *omono* contrast with *iJEno* in that the first two indicate male kinsmen in this group while the latter indicates female kinsmen. *Omono* contrasts with *ahono* in separating mother's male siblings from father's male siblings.

The next contrastive group is much more complex. It contrasts with the first group in that the terms designate only kinsmen of ego's own generation or a generation junior to ego's. On one side is the single term *noho.* It refers to kinsmen to whom ego traces a relationship through a sibling of opposite sex or a pair of siblings of opposite sex to each other. Assuming a male ego, a *noho* could be a sister's child or a father's sister's child. For the sake of convenience we will say these are kinsmen joined to ego by asymmetrical links. On the other side is a group of four terms contrasting with *noho* because they refer to kinsmen related to ego through a pair of siblings of the same sex or to ego's own siblings. These four terms contrast with one another on the basis of sex and relative age. Thus, *atEno* refers to a female in this group older than ego, and *aru'nE* to a female younger than ego. Similarly, *uBono* refers to a male older than ego, and *naku'nE* to a male younger than ego. We will refer to these kinsmen as joined to ego by symmetrical links.

The final group contrasts with the others because it only refers to kinsmen of generations junior to ego's. The terms *gipE'nE* and *arunE* designate ego's own children plus the children of anyone related to ego through symmetrical links with the first term applied to males and the second to females. These two terms apply to kinsmen one generation below ego, while the term *na'Bo* applies to kinsmen linked in the same way but removed from ego by two descending generations. These three terms contrast with the term *gwo'mo* because it refers to the children of anyone related to ego through asymmetrical links one or more generations below ego.

There are other, more complex ways of discovering what characteristics of the genealogical relationship between ego and alter are being taken into account in the various classes of kinsmen designated by the kin terms. Even this relatively simple analysis, however, indicates the importance of certain principles such as distinguishing between generational levels, symmetrical as opposed to asymmetrical links, sex, and relative age. Once these characteristics are discovered they can be used as clues in further research. For example, the separation of cross cousins from parallel cousins and the identification of mother's brother by a special term suggest the existence of social groups in which unilineal descent is an organizational principle. Further, the development of a terminology to distinguish between ego's own siblings and the children of ego's parents' siblings on the basis of relative age alerts us to the possibility that authority in kin-based groups may depend on differences in age among kinsmen of the same generational level as well as between generational levels.

The genealogies can be put to a number of other uses as well. Some basic demographic data can be tabulated from them, such as the range and average number of children born to a married couple, the number of infant deaths, and the population pyramid for a given community. They also provide clues concerning various aspects of the marriage pattern. From the Miruma genealogies it is evident that about 10 percent of the marriages are polygynous; the levirate is practiced, but rare; there are no spinsters, but about 4 percent of the men are bachelors; and more wives come from inside the tribe than from outside it. There are also indications in the genealogies that marriage is a difficult adjustment for girls. The first wife of 63 percent of the males in Miruma and the second wife of 40 percent ran away from her husband or was sent away by him because of her recalcitrance.

One of the more interesting classes of material evident in the Miruma genealogies relates to causes of death. No systematic attempt was made in this instance to collect statements concerning the cause of death of all those reported on the genealogies as deceased, but informants frequently volunteered the information. As the material accumulated it became evident that young married women frequently committed suicide at the death of their husbands, and that a large proportion of nonsuicidal deaths were described to the malevolent attacks of sorcerers and ghosts. Neither of these facts is meaningful by itself, but they suggest lines of further investigation.

The genealogies in combination with the census of a village provide initial insight into the composition of this residential unit. One can trace the precise kin links between the various families in the village, one can detect what kinds of kinsmen tend to stay in the village, what kinds tend to move out, and by identifying those individuals or families living in the village that are not kinsmen of some kind, one can ascertain what factors operate to bring nonkinsmen into the village. Some of the results of this investigation will be presented in the next chapter.

3

Focusing on Groups

"They are the ones that sit down together."

A STRANGER soon discovers that while living with a particular household or village he is expected to participate in certain kinds of activities with others of the same unit, he may be excluded from participating in similar activities when they are carried out in another unit of the same order. So too, the ethnographer finds the world divided by "we" and "they" and, further, that the referent of "we" varies from one situation to another. He tries to find out how people organize themselves for tasks and events, and how they decide who is an "insider" and who an "outsider" in various circumstances. The ethnographer focuses his attention on social groups early in the field study, especially those that maintain their identity over a long period of time, control some kind of property, or exhibit other characteristics of corporateness.

Identifying Groups

Discovering the social groups that make up a society can begin with a map and census for these show significant concentrations of people and one can usually safely assume that such concentrations represent relatively stable groups of some kind. The map of the upper Asaro valley shows a series of bays and narrower valleys with villages clustered in them. Each of these areas is separated from its neighbor by large, unoccupied ridges or stretches of open grassland, and each area tends to be treated as a unit in that a single name, or a pair of names, is given to the people living in it. Thus, people from the village of Miruma will point to the valley north of them and say, "There are Mandu-Amoso," or to the valley south of them and say, "There are Kofena-Ka'nasa." Similarly, people living in either of these areas will point to the bay containing the village of Miruma and say, "There are Gururumba-FikEsE." In the Gururumba-FikEsE area people are seldom heard to refer to themselves by either of these names, but if they do, it is usually by one or the other rather than both.

27

Furthermore, whole villages are either Gururumba or FikEsE, and a line can be drawn on an enlarged map of this bay separating all villages referred to by one of these names from all referred to by the other. This use of names presumably indicates some kind of territorial grouping. Collecting the names used by the people of each bay to refer to all the others produces a consistent list of names revealing fourteen such groups in the upper Asaro valley. In five instances the names are paired while in four they are not.

Miruma is a Gururumba village, but when people there talk of "we" or "us" in some large sense they do not usually mean Miruma and all other Gururumba villages. Asking them the rather ambiguous question, "What large group do you belong to?" most frequently elicits the answer, "Wa'muJuhu." The referent of this name is also a grouping with a territorial base, for in addition to Miruma it includes the two new villages on either side of it and the surrounding land where almost all the gardens of these villages are located. Similarly, the names AsErE'Juhu and KafindE'Juhu group the remaining Gururumba villages into two additional units having territorial identity. The common ending *Juhu* on these names is interesting and also occurs in the names Gwonambu'-Juhu, GulifE'Juhu, and LonohoNgu'Juhu for groups of neighboring FikEsE villages. *Juhu* means "dried seed." Its connotation is not that of potential growth or of inability to grow, but of established growth. Thus, the names ending in *Juhu* appear to indicate territorially discreet subdivisions of larger territorial units that have achieved some identity through time as well as on the ground.

Indication of another kind of unit with territorial identity is given on maps of villages. As mentioned above, the large, new villages are divided by transverse fences with a men's house in each segment. These segments can be referred to by the name of the plot of ground where they are located, or by the phrases "the uphills" and "the downhills" depending on their relative position on the ridge.

Map and census cannot by themselves tell us much more about the social groups characterizing this society. An additional bit of negative information is the lack of a name for all the people living in the upper Asaro as distinct from all those of the lower Asaro except the phrases "the uphills" and "the downhills." Whether or not the "uphills" form a social unit, and what identifies other named groups in addition to their territoriality, are questions that must be answered with material beyond that already considered. Groups must be identified as they are revealed in concrete assemblies of people. Observations must therefore await the occurrence of events and situations that generate such assemblies.

In an alien situation one learns that it is not always possible to tell when concrete assemblies of people are acting as members of groups or when they are a heterogeneous set of persons brought together by circumstance. In order to proceed with the business of gathering data the ethnographer makes certain assumptions that he hopes will guide him to those assemblies of people that manifest group identity. This is a justifiable procedure as long as he realizes the assumptions he is making. For example, I regularly assumed I was really seeing a group acting whenever visitors to Miruma stopped outside the village and arranged themselves into a compact formation before entering the village. I assumed that entering the village en masse was a deliberate act accentuating group identity. This assumption proved to be a reliable one, but I also assumed the interaction of groups whenever I saw a fight involving several people taking place in the presence of an audience that seemed to be arranged in "sides." This assumption proved to be unreliable in the sense that sometimes it was correct and sometimes it was not. The most reliable and consistently used assumption was that group identities were involved whenever food was publicly distributed in the context of an assembly divided into givers and recipients.

The purpose of identifying those assemblies of people that seem to represent social groups are to observe their activities in order to learn what kinds of affairs are managed by groups and to observe their personnel to learn what criteria of membership are employed. The village of Miruma became a kind of sociological benchmark in gathering data of this kind. All the people having houses there or regularly coming into one of the men's houses were known to me. For the whole period of the field study records were kept of the way these people divided themselves or joined together in various kinds of activities. Because it was physically impossible to watch all of them all the time, the records represent only a sample, but an attempt was made to check this validity by hiring several young boys to report daily on the activities of four or five adult males. This provided a complete picture of the way the men of this village arranged themselves for the more routine affairs of daily life. In addition to looking for data relevant to the internal divisions of Miruma, data was also sought on the way Miruma joined other villages to form larger groupings. For example, its common participation with villages designated Wa'muJuhu as guests of host villages called GulifE'Juhu became part of this data.

It may happen, of course, that one never sees certain social groups as concrete entities. Some kinds of groups only manifest themselves through representatives; others never assemble because the rights and obligations entailed in group membership do not involve it; still others find no occasion for assemblies during the observer's stay. Therefore, some groups are only "seen" as analytic constructs or through the descriptive accounts of informants, and identification of them may not occur until after the ethnographer returns from the field.

Identifying groups by seeing them in concrete assembly attests to their existence but does not identify their membership criteria. To discover these criteria the ethnographer attempts to find some features common to all the people participating in the activities of named social units or the assemblies he thinks may be social groups. Here again assumptions are made in order to start data collection. For example, my first assumption was that kinship would be an important criterion and viewed every assembly of people or named unit as bounded in some way by kinship. Discovering when this assumption was not warranted was my first step in discovering other membership criteria.

Over a period of time a body of knowledge is accumulated about groups by locating named entities on the ground, observing concrete assemblies, and finding the membership criteria of assumed social groups. There is a final area of information that may also help in the discovery process, although the degree of its usefulness varies a great deal from one culture to another. This is the understanding people themselves have of the system of groups into which they are organized. They may have terms for different kinds of groups, as in the terms "family," "state," "nation," "club," or "corporation" from our own culture. They may have explanations of group structure or accounts of how the current arrangement of groups came to be. Not much of this kind of information was available, for the people did not seem to have speculated much about the inner workings of their own society. What they did say will be reported in the following sections.

Who Are the Gururumba?

The name "Gururumba" appears in the title of this book and has been mentioned in a previous section. What kind of group is this? How does it articulate with similar groups or differ from others? The Gururumba will be the immediate referent for the rest of the book because most of the observations on which it is based were made among them rather than similarly constituted groups in the area.

The question "who are the Gururumba" can be answered as if one were describing the physical properties of an object. The name designates 1121 people living in six large villages in the northern half of a large bay on the west side of the upper Asaro valley. It designates a territorially distinct unit of approximately thirty square miles in the sense that none of these six villages, nor any of the gardens belonging to people living in the villages, are outside this territory. The people living inside this territory see themselves as a unified entity indicating a more complex group than one characterized solely by territorial discreetness. The name not only designates an "it" but also a "who," and in the minds of non-Gururumba it designates "those people standing opposed to us" and not simply "people of that place."

The people called Gururumba apply this name to themselves and, in addition, point up their existence as a unified entity by explaining how they came to be. There is a story telling of a time when the upper Asaro valley was largely uninhabited. People from the lower valley made excursions into it to hunt and gather, but they did not live there. Those who used it most frequently lived in a large village (the name of which has been forgotten) on the edge of this region which was at that time covered with forest. One day a fight broke out in this village because a man killed a pregnant woman for stealing some mushrooms he had been saving for his supper. The fight divided the village into several warring factions each of which moved off into a part of the upper valley as a defensive measure. They remained there, planted gardens, flourished, and became part of the present population. The Gururumba were one of these groups. This story may not provide us much actual history, but it does tell us that the Gururumba think of themselves as a social unit in existence over a long period of time.

Other aspects of this story inform us about the internal structure of this group. To the ethnographer schooled in working with societies where kinship is an important structural feature, it is interesting that this story does not depict the factionalization of the village along descent group lines. It was not brother against brother or the descendants of one man against the descendants of another who formed the factions generated by the killing. As the story depicts them, these factions were those residents in a village who took common cause in a dispute, and although they may have been kinsmen the story makes the point irrelevant by exclusion. This detail of the story mirrors the fact that although the Gururumba consider themselves to be the descendants of a common set of ancestors, these ancestors are not specifically known nor do they form a descent group among themselves. The ancestors are simply the original group to occupy this territory and defend it against outsiders. Similarly, the Gururumba are the present day descendants of this heterogeneous group who remain committed to common defense of the territory.

The cohesiveness of this group, which we will call a phratry, derives primarily from occupying a common territory, acting in common defense, and feeling a continuity with the past. The authority structure in the phratry may be regarded as a secondary source of cohesion, for none of the three primary sources is utilized by the Gururumba to devise rules specifying positions of central authority. There is no phratry head picked generation after generation from the occupants of one village, the ranks of hereditary war leaders, or some particular descent line. In fact, one seldom finds a single, dominant leader of an Asaro phratry. As we will see below, becoming a leader means becoming a man of renown, and this is a complex process requiring men of certain temperament and skill. The extent of a man's influence is dependent on his renown, and the phratry can be regarded as the largest unit within which a man of renown can influence others on matters of policy. Thus, strong central authority in the phratry depends on the existence in it of a man with greater renown than all others. Since this does not usually occur, authority comes to be shared among several men.

The authority structure itself is not so much a source of cohesion as is the fact that the phratry is considered a field of action for reaching a settlement in matters under dispute. This is exemplified in the notion of two kinds of warfare. One is called *roBo,* warring with deadly weapons such as spears, axes, and arrows. The other is called *nande,* fighting with sticks, stones, and hands. In addition, *roBo* connotes fighting with the intent to decimate the enemy, while *nande* connotes fighting that can be halted short of extensive killing or property destruction and, further, that a settlement of the dispute giving rise to the fight can be reached by nonviolent means. It is said that people of different phratries war (*roBo*) with one another, while people of the same phratry only fight (*nande*). The phratry, then, is not the group in which one finds the authority to which disputes can be referred for final adjudication, it is simply the group within which people are willing to admit the possibility of an amicable settlement of a dispute.

Just as the group has not used the sources of cohesion of the phratry, which we have broadly defined, to build a separable authority structure within it, neither has it utilized them to rigidify the boundaries between "insiders" and "outsiders." Whole groups may be incorporated into the phratry by moving onto its territory and agreeing to defend it. For example, one of the Gururumba villages is made up entirely of people from the Chimbu valley who speak a different language, wear different costume, and are culturally different in other ways. They were invited by the Gururumba to come as a unit and settle there with the understanding they would help defend it, and although they have not been in the area long enough to lose their identity they are in the process of doing so. In other words, "continuity with the past" is not based on the notion of the past as a specifically defined segment of time but as something being continually created, and "occupying a common territory" does not imply a boundary that never changes.

To this point, the phratry has been considered as an entity appearing on the ground, as a field of political action, and as a unit in warfare. It also appears as a unit within which certain kinds of activities carried out by its constituent parts are coordinated, and as a unit in a religious ritual. The two main activities coordinated within the phratry are the pig festival and grass-burning for hunting purposes. The pig festival is a large-scale ceremony occurring at intervals of five or more years and involving many hundreds of people. If a phratry is large, like the Gururumba, the festival is organized and implemented by the parts of the phratry we will come to know as sibs rather than by the phratry itself. In such a case there is agreement that the various sibs should hold their ceremonies seriatim over a brief period of time rather than all at the same time or at irregular intervals. Therefore, the complex arrangements entailed in the ceremony have to be coordinated among the sibs. When the sequence will begin and what the order of precedence will be must be decided on the phratry level; this is done by agreement and mutual consent rather than by dictation or traditional rule. The grass-burning is no longer done on a large scale because the lowland grass area is now being used for gardens, but in former times the grass was frequently fired in order to drive the rodents and other small animals living there into the open where they could be caught in large numbers. Coordination was utilized here to control the fire and maximize the catch.

In addition to these coordinated activities the phratry appears as a unit in a religious ritual called the *jaBirisi*. This takes place around a fenced enclosure located near the center of the phratry territory and occurs during times of crisis. Representatives from each village of the phratry are the main actors in this ritual, but they act as a unit in directing the ritual to the ancestral group which gave rise to the phratry.

The Larger Picture

The Gururumba are part of two larger kinds of units. The first of these will be called a tribe and designates named units like the two phratries Gururumba-FikEsE. This tribe occupies the land of a single bay, numbers approximately 2300 people, and is distributed among ten new villages. Warfare (*roBo*) may break out within the tribe but the two phratries do not regard one another as traditional enemies. Furthermore, neither one will combine with an outside group to attack the other. They may not aid the other in defense against such an attack, but neither will they contribute to the efforts of the enemy. The story concerning the origin of the Gururumba mentioned in the preceding section states that the FikEsE were living in the area before the Gururumba entered it. The two phratries are thus depicted as deriving from different ancestral groups. It will be recalled that ten of the fourteen phratries in the upper Asaro valley are linked in named pairs of this nature. In each case, one of the members of the pair is said to have come from the original dispersion mentioned in the story and the other from some other background. The Ka'nasa of KofEna-Ka'-nasa are said to have come from the Siane area to the southwest; the Mandu of Mandu-Amoso from Chimbu; the AnaNgu of KErEmu-AnaNgu from over the mountains to the northeast; and the LunEmbe of LunEmbe-Gifukoni from another part of the lower Asaro. Some of these groups are said to have been in the area at the time of the dispersion and some to have come after it. All this evidence indicates that the unit we are calling a tribe is a political alliance of long standing between two phratries occupying what they consider to be a common territory. This distinguishes the tribe as a unit from short-term alliances formed between phratries outside these territorial blocks. Thus, the Gururumba now consider the KErEmu their allies, but the KErEmu are outside the Gururumba-FikEsE territorial block; they were enemies as a result of the incident related in the origin story; it is expected the alliance will not continue for long; the alliance is recent; and a common name is never applied to the two groups.

This analysis implies either that the phratries that do not occur in pairs are coterminous with a tribe, and there are fourteen tribes in the valley, or that a tribe represents a degree of political integration not achieved by all phratries, thus making five tribes and four phratries in the valley. The latter interpretation seems preferable since although tribes do not perform any activities that phratries do not also perform, they are a more complex grouping.

The Gururumba are part of a second kind of unit defined primarily on cultural grounds consisting of all the people in the upper Asaro valley. No name is applied to this unit, but the recognition of its existence is embodied in the statement that all these people are "of one leaf." This statement has a double connotation, for it indicates they all eat the same kind of food and also that they all use the same kinds of plants in various magical manipulations. Linguistic differences are also recognized in a relative as well as an absolute sense, so that dialectical differences between upper Asaro and lower Asaro are not equated with the greater degree of difference between Asaro speakers and Siane speakers. Chimbu speakers, with a remotely related language, are put in another class. Other cultural features they see as distinctive to themselves include items of dress, the use of a sacred object called a geruna board, and certain songs and dances. If the actual distribution of any of these traits were plotted on a map one would see that while they are not distinctive to the upper Asaro valley, their particular constellation is.

The unit defined by this constellation of cultural traits and by the geographical boundaries of the upper valley is the world the people living there know most intimately. It is the territory they most frequently walk over, it contains the groups they most frequently fight with, most mates are found within it, all myths and tales refer to happenings within its boundaries, and the lines of economic exchange focus in on it. We regard it as a unit, then, because it is the effective center of the social world for any person in it, and is so recognized by the people themselves.

The Smaller Picture

The Gururumba are made up of smaller units. The first of these is apparent to the outsider because it is geographically distinct and because it is named in a peculiar way, adding *Juhu* as a suffix to its name. Every phratry examined has at least two of these as constituent parts, and the Gururumba have three. The term "sib" will be used to refer to these groups. There is no native term for this kind of group, but in attempting to explain its character to the ethnographer people will frequently say, "They are the ones who sit down together," or, "They are like brothers." The first statement refers to the fact that when this group acts as a unit vis-à-vis other units, as in a food distribution, they sit together during the proceedings. The phratry and the tribe never manifest themselves in this way. The second statement refers to the fact that all members of a sib think of themselves as a descent group. In one case the group is explained in terms of visibility and in the other in terms of membership criterion.

The sib appears as a unit in a much larger number of activities than the phratry or tribe. It arranges and executes the pig festival mentioned above. If food is particularly plentiful in a given year it will hold a food distribution very similar to the pig festival in its intent and structure except that sugar cane, taro, and yams are the foods involved; it is somewhat smaller in scale, and it does not have the religious overtones of the pig festival. The sib also appears as guest group at these occasions to perform spectacular dances and little dramas full of subtle humor or surprising effects. Its members may appear as mourners or the bereaved in funeral ceremonies, but this is partially dependent on other factors. The sib was the basic unit in warfare before the Australian influence and larger war parties were made up of several sibs individually agreeing to participate with the instigating sib in the action. Ceremonial labor, as when the first garden plot is cleared for a newly married couple, is carried out by the sib as a unit, and the new government-imposed work on the roads is organized by sibs.

In addition to appearing as a unit, the sib becomes visible through its members' exercise of obligations and rights that produce actions outside the context of an assembled group. Thus, a man may recruit aides from among his sib mates to avenge a close kinsman's death by killing some member of the killer's sib. Any man from one sib may call any man from another sib by the kin term *niJimo* (affine) if any man in the one is married to any woman of the other. If a man kills a member of another sib, whatever the circumstances he can expect that his own sib mates will not regard it as a punishable act, in most instances defending him against attempts of the other sib to punish him. If he kills a member of his own sib, however, he must defend himself. The sib is also the widest exogamous unit since mates can be found in any sib except one's own.

The term "sib" designates social groups whose membership is defined by descent, although the actual genealogical links between all the members cannot be traced. This is the case, for example, with the Gururumba sib named Wa'mu-Juhu. The Wa'muJuhu say they are descended from a pair of brothers, but the names of the brothers are not known, and no one knows who is descended from the elder brother and who from the younger. Common descent is implied rather than actual. The imputation of common descent means that all one's sib mates are, in a general way, regarded as consanguineal kinsmen. This is evident in the fact that terms used to refer to consanguineals can be extended to sib mates as terms of address; this is rarely done for members of other sibs in the phratry. The appropriate term is selected on the basis of the sex and age of the referent rather than a calculated consanguineal link. Thus, any very old man or woman in ego's sib may be addressed by the terms "father" or "mother," any slightly older man or woman as "elder brother" or "elder sister," and so on. The rule of descent in the sib is patrilineal as indicated by the facts that the ancestors of the sib are always depicted as males, and the extended families comprising the sib are linked together in patrilineages.

The patrilineages comprising a sib are not spread evenly over the sib territory; they occur in the clumps recognizable as villages. These villages are not simply genealogical subdivisions of the sib, however, for if they were, one would expect that all the lineages in the village would see themselves as descended from some ancestor who was in turn descended from the sib ancestor by some known link. Looking at the genealogies from any Gururumba village shows this is simply not the case. Villages may contain from six to fifteen lineages and even in small villages no common ancestor is cited except the remote and unknown sib ancestor. It is significant in this connection that the members of different patrilineages living together in the same village do not usually use kin terms to refer to or address one another. Personal names and teknonymy are used instead. This indicates the village is not the same kind of unit as the sib, differing perhaps only in scale. This is further supported by the fact that the village includes people who would be excluded if it were based on the same principle as the patrisib. In a patrilineal descent group all descendents of the female members of the group and all persons who are not connected to it through consanguineal links are systematically excluded but in a Gururumba village one finds people, of precisely these types living there and participating in its affairs. For example, the wives of all the men claiming descent from the sib ancestor are persons not connected to the sib through consanguineal links for the sib is exogamous and wives usually leave their natal sib at marriage to live with their husband in a village of his sib. Asking wives of Miruma men if they are Wa'muJuhu usually elicits a negative response accompanied by the naming of their natal sib, and observing their behavior indicates they have not given up membership in their own sib for they may move back to it and activate their property rights at any time. In addition to wives, the village contains other people not members of the sib. These include affines more distant than wives, matrilineally related kinsmen, and men from other tribes. The first two types have some kin link to at least one lineage in the village, but the last is there by agreement only or because they are married to lineage women and reside with their wives' lineage rather than their own. Virilocal residence is the most frequently occurring form of residence, but uxorilocal residence also occurs and it is not viewed as deviant or unusual. Of the fifty-three married couples with children in the village of Miruma, fifteen, or 28 percent fall into these three categories.

If the village were only a collecting point for people, there would be no problem in specifying the relationship of village to sib. The wives and others would be nonsib members residing with sib members. A problem arises, however, because the village is itself a social unit in that it has an internal structure, a sense of identity indicated by the use of a village name, and activities not performed by other units. The inhabitants of a village frequently act as a unit in court cases; they move into the forest during a certain time of the year to gather pandanus nuts; they perform a ritual to insure the future growth of pandanus nuts; they may act as guest or host in a food distribution; and they are a unit in one form of ceremonial courtship. Funerals are usually a function of the sib, but if a person dies while living in a village not part of his or her own sib, the village organizes the funeral. The village is also the most important unit in negotiating bride price and all subsequent exchanges between the bride's group and the groom's group. All village residents are potential contributors to the price for in-marrying women and are all potential recipients of the price given for out-marrying women. The internal structure of the village consists of a division into wards each of which centers around a different men's house.

The village, then, can be thought of as a unit recruiting some of its members on the basis of patrilineal descent, which makes it a localized segment of a sib, and on the basis of several other criteria as well. Since the most frequently employed of these other criteria is a rule of residence operating to move most wives into their husbands villages, the village will be classified as a clan or compromise kin group as defined by Murdock.[1] It can then be said that the relationship between sib and clan is such that sib membership depends on birth and

[1] George Peter Murdock, *Social Structure,* New York, The Macmillan Company, 1949.

cannot be changed while clan membership may depend on either birth or residence and changes whenever residence changes. Lineages are composed of sib mates recognizing a known, common ancestor, and wards are all those extended families in a clan whose adult males belong to the same men's house. In this conceptualization, lineages are subdivisions of sibs, and wards are subdivisions of clans.

Some further observations help demonstrate the relationship between sib and clan. In any village most of the men are members of the same sib and most of the women are of various other sibs. There are a few women, however, who are of the same sib as most of the men. These are sib sisters whose husbands have taken up uxorilocal rather than virilocal residence. There is an observable difference in the degree to which these two classes of women are allowed to voice their opinion concerning public affairs. In the village of Miruma those few women who are Wa'muJuhu are occasionally allowed to stand in court cases or other public gatherings where issues are being decided and speak in an attempt to influence decisions. The majority of women, who are clan mates but not sib mates, are usually enjoined to remain silent or speak only on points of information. Also, these Wa'mu Juhu women are residing with their natal lineage, and when they become old they may be allowed to become guardians of a sacred object identified with the lineage and with the men's secret cult. The other women are not allowed to do this and, supposedly, do not even know the object exists. Again, Wa'muJuhu women residing with a clan of their natal sib more frequently become leaders of women's activities than do other women. One final observation concerning the relationship between sib and clan focuses on the descendents of those men who are members of a clan but not the sib of which it is a localized segment. If a man resides most of his life in a clan not of his own sib, his descendents become members of the clan sib rather than his natal sib. This can happen in one generation although it usually takes at least two. Putting this observation alongside the fact that the sib is a group where kinship is imputed rather than actual leads one to the supposition that a sib grows through the incorporation of ousiders as well as the expansion and division of the lineages within it.

Other Kinds of Groups

The groups discussed so far have been defined by culture traits, political alliance, territoriality, descent, and residence. They form a series of greater inclusiveness based on combinations of these criteria. There are other kinds of groups that do not fit this series and two of them will be mentioned here. The first was identified through discovering the meaning of the word *ambo*. Men were observed calling one another *ambo* and referring to one another as "my *ambo*" or "his *ambo*." The term did not appear to be a kin term because it was never elicited while collecting a genealogy. The first meaning offered for it was "men born on the same day." This did not seem true because it was used between men of different ages. Subsequent investigation revealed that it designated all men initiated at the same time into the men's cult. This initiation takes place at irregular intervals and may include boys as young as ten or eleven and as old as fifteen or sixteen years, thus accounting for the discrepancy in age. The reference to birth is intended to indicate sociological rather than biological birth, for the initiation moves a boy from the status of child to the status of unmarried adult. We will translate the term as "age mate" because the relationship between one group of *ambo* and another is thought of by the people as similar to the relationship between an older and a younger group of siblings. Because the initiation is sometimes performed by the sib and sometimes by the clan, a man may or may not have age mates in other clans. If he does he is regarded as fortunate, since age mates are as friends and quite responsive to one another's needs. They support one another in arguments, help in subsistence activities, and stand together in dance groups. To have someone in another clan who will do these things "spontaneously" is regarded as an advantage. Age mates appear most conspicuously as a unit during the initiation itself and the long period of Spartan living following it. In later years they do not appear as an assembled unit, but can be seen analytically as constituting a field of friendship.

The second kind of grouping uses sex as the criterion of membership and produces the two groups "men" and "women." It is debatable whether or not these divisions can be called social groups in the strictest sense of the term, but it is at least interesting to think of them in this way. Men are organized into a secret cult from which women are excluded. The women have no comparable cult, but they stand, as a unit, in opposition to men in various contexts. For example, men own pigs, but women carry out the day-to-day tending of them. A woman is spoken of as the "mother" of the pigs she tends, and when they are killed she mourns them. If large numbers of pigs are killed for exchange purposes, there may be an organized stickfight between all the women and the men who have become "killers" of their "children." The men's cult is organized around the playing of sacred flutes kept secret from women, but myths relate that these flutes once belonged to women who revealed them to men. Women carry out some rituals associated with first menstruation, betrothal, and birth, from which men are excluded. There is residential segregation by sex after puberty. This grouping by sex does not crosscut all other groups, so that men do not stand as a unit against women on the tribe, phratry, or sib level. It does crosscut the clan and ward, however.

4

Focusing on Roles

". . . so Elder Sister carried Younger Brother away."

ISCOVERING HOW PEOPLE organize themselves for certain tasks and events as "insiders" and "outsiders" locates points of reference for the stranger. A particular set of rights, duties, and attitudes becomes associated with a particular set of membership criteria. Other sets of rights, duties, and attitudes are associated with kinds of persons rather than kinds of groups. When the ethnologist begins to think about a human group in this way he tries to see it as a set of relationships between socially defined persons who behave toward one another in expected ways. He applies the concept of role to bring the situation into focus. Information contributing to the discovery of these patterns comes from a wide variety of sources: observing consistencies in behavior, eliciting statements concerning how certain categories of persons ought to act toward others, attending disputes arising from unfulfilled expectations, and even examining myths and tales that recount the deeds of people standing in particular relationships to one another.

Before the ethnographer can begin systematically collecting information from any of these sources, however, he must identify the various kinds of social persons recognized by the people he is studying. In an alien culture this process of recognition proceeds rather slowly for although the ethnographer can comfortably assume that some roles will be organized around differences essentially similar to those he knows from his own culture, he must also assume that there are recognized differences that will not appear familiar to him. In all known cultures distinctive patterns of behavior are built around the sexual dichotomy and around differences in age. These differences are relatively easy to observe visually and provide a convenient starting point for the ethnographer. All known cultures also have distinctive patterns of behavior built around differences in degrees of kinship, but these differences are not so easy to observe visually. A mother's brother does not look any different than a father's brother; hence the ethnographer must rely on his knowledge of the distinctions inherent in the system of kinship terminology to tell him whether or not such a pair is regarded as one social person or two.

The ethnographer may also easily assume that there will be recognized differences in prestige or in task specialization, but recognizing these differences entails difficulties because the visual cues marking them are unknown to him initially, and because, in a society like the Gururumba, these cues are not usually elaborately developed. There are, for example, prestigeful men in Gururumba society, but their dress and style of life is almost indistinguishable from that of their less prestigeful fellows. Similarly, there is some task specialization beyond that organized around differences in sex and age, but these specialists wear no distinctive uniform nor are they so occupied with their specialty that their activity pattern stands conspicuously apart from the activity pattern of others.

In this chapter I will examine some of the roles characteristic of Gururumba society and some of the ways the ethnographer becomes aware of them.

Men and Women

The Gururumba have two words, *EvEnE* and *vEnE,* that correspond closely in meaning to our words, *man* and *woman.* They designate a pair of roles contrasting with one another in terms of sex but linked with one another through the shared characteristic of adulthood. Casual observation is sufficient to reveal some of the rights and duties defining these roles. This is most obvious with respect to duties that have a tasklike quality. Certain tasks are allocated to men, others to women; this can be discovered by watching the daily routine around the village and in the gardens. In the garden, for example, men plant and tend sugar cane, bananas, taro, and yams, while women are responsible for sweet potatoes (the staple crop) and a wide variety of green vegetables. Men break the soil in a new garden, build the fence, and dig the drainage ditches, while women prepare the initially broken soil and do almost all the weeding. In house building men perform all phases of planning and construction except the cutting and carrying of thatch, which is left to the women. Both men and women prepare food for daily consumption, but only men engineer the preparation and cooking of large amounts of food in earth ovens for festive occasions. Men kill, castrate, loan, give, and trade pigs, while women tend to their daily care and feeding. Men cut and carry wood, while women dig and carry sweet potatoes. There are some tasks that men and women alike perform, such as tending the fire or boiling food, but for the most part the work activities of the two sexes are complementary rather than parallel.

Some kinds of rights characteristic of these roles are also fairly easy to observe. Attending court cases and minor disputes makes it clear that men and women have different kinds of rights over various classes of property. Men exercise ultimate control over land and the usable products on it. For example, a woman planted a pandanus nut tree on her husband's land when she first married him and tried to claim the nuts from the tree after she divorced him. She lost the case because, although she had planted and tended the tree for many years, it was on his land. Women sometimes argue with their husbands over pandanus nuts because the wife wants to send nuts to her consanguineal relatives while the husband wants to allocate them in another way. The woman invariably loses if the issue is decided in terms of legalistic rights. In fact, there is very little property over which a woman can exercise final control except her implements, clothing, ornaments, and a few spells or charms associated with garden magic. She has rights of usufruct over land, dwellings, or patches of forest containing usable plants that are contingent upon her marriage or family affiliation, but she has no rights of alienation over any of these things for that right rests with men—either individually or in groups.

The enumeration of rights and duties could be continued, but doing so would ignore the fact that in Gururumba culture the roles *EvEnE* and *vEnE* are more than a bundle of rights and duties associated with limited areal activity. In some degree they pattern almost all sectors of an individual's life, and the relationship between them is one of the most important recognized by the Gururumba. For example, examination of the inventory of roles reveals that the majority of roles are appropriate to one sex or the other but not both. Almost all the recognized categories of kinsmen are appropriate to only one sex, so that the kinds of kinsman a person can be are fundamentally different for men and for women. Furthermore, the kinds of roles an individual can play beyond the kinship system are quite different for men and for women. The difference lies primarily in the fact that men can play a wider variety of roles than women. A man can become a warrior, a person of renown and influence, or a curer. Women can become none of these things nor is there a parallel set of roles to which they have access. It is clear, then, that the roles *EvEnE* and *vEnE* are very general roles; that being one or the other largely determines a person's total life pattern in so far as it is structured by roles.

It is in the area of ritual and supernaturalism that the importance of the relationship between these two roles is most striking. It is also the area where the ethnographer acquires knowledge slowly and, occasionally, in unexpected ways. Early in the field study it became apparent that Gururumba men were puzzled by certain aspects of the relationship between my wife and myself. Specifically, they expressed concern over the fact that night after night I slept in the same house with my wife and, indeed, in the same room. It developed that their concern was for my general health and physical well-being. The connection between these two things was not apparent to me and direct questioning on the subject elicited only vague answers to the effect that prolonged cohabitation with a woman should be avoided because it would leave one physically weak or susceptible to illness. While this information was not in itself particularly enlightening, it did set me to compiling a list of prohibitions and avoidances relating to contact between men and women in the hope that it might shed some light on the problem. I found, for example, that a woman should not touch a man's bow, a man should not accept food from the hand of a menstruating woman, a woman should not touch the drinking tube of a man while menstruating, a man should not have sexual relations the day before undertaking a difficult task, a woman should destroy all traces of menstrual blood lest a man come in contact with it, and a young man should avoid any contact with his wife-to-be until he has a fully grown beard. Failure to practice these avoidances and others like them was said to result in illness, weakness or, in some cases, death. Observation of Gururumba behavior demonstrated that these avoidances were in fact followed very closely in daily life.

Other facts discovered from time to time seemed relevant to this general pattern. On certain ceremonial occasions the men played pairs of bamboo flutes in the gardens and forests around the village. Since they believe these flutes embody the power of growth and fertility, playing them induced growth. Women do not take part in this activity and, in fact, are debarred from seeing the flutes. Moreover, women are encouraged to believe that the sound produced by the flutes is the cry of a mystic bird. However, a seeming paradox is found in a myth explaining the origin of these flutes. The myth relates that the flutes and their power were revealed to a young man by a woman who eventually changed into a small animal, thus leaving the secret of the flutes with men rather than women. In another ritual, that of male initiation, boys are made to vomit and sweat in order to remove contaminating substances from their bodies accumulated through contact with their mothers. Also, blood is made to flow from their noses, an act said to be equivalent to menstruation. These things are done in the initiation, it is said, in order to make the young boys grow and develop physically. Further, the Gururumba believe that childbirth, or anything associated with it, is dangerous to men. Thus, there is a ceremony soon after childbirth designed to indicate whether or not the father's physical strength has been impaired by the birth. There is a prohibition against a man eating any of the food prepared for the feast announcing the first pregnancy of his wife because this feast is associated with childbirth. This proscription even extends to all a man's age mates if they are not themselves fathers.

These various items of ritual and belief indicate the roles $EvEnE$ and $vEnE$ constitute a relationship thought to have a far-reaching and fundamental influence on human affairs. This influence appears to stem from the difference in sexual functioning between men and women, but the Gururumba see its effects in more generalized terms than are inherent in the biological distinction. Controlling the relationship between men and women is equated with controlling physical well-being and growth in the broadest terms. These roles, then, are not only connected with the organization of tasks or the definition of rights, they are also connected with ideas concerning the basic causative forces in the world. What these forces are and how they operate will be described at greater length in succeeding sections.

Leaders

In describing our arrival in the village of Miruma I mentioned that the government medical officer charged two men in authority with looking after our welfare. These were the *luluai* and *tultul,* government-appointed native officials. These roles are important, but they will not be considered at this point because they are a product of the contact situation and not a part of the aboriginal role system. Even the names of these roles, which come from Neo-Melanesian, are not native names. The role to be discussed here is designated by the term *EvEnE nambo,* "big man." It was not difficult to identify the men who play this role because they were pointed out to me almost casually during the first few weeks of the field study. At gatherings where important matters were being discussed or while walking with a group of people from one place to another someone would simply indicate one of the assembled group and say, "Luiso is a big man," or "Those two are big men." Men's houses were consistently referred to as the house of a particular individual, followed by the comment that the person in question was a "big man." In the context of group discussions the men so designated were observed to open and close discussions and to make longer, somewhat more involved speeches than other men. It seemed clear that this term designated some kind of leadership role, and therefore those men referred to in this way were observed over a long period of time in various contexts to determine the nature of the role.

In the course of daily affairs "big men" are not particularly noticeable. They tend to be in their late thirties or forties but not much older. Their dress is not distinctive except on ceremonial occasions when they appear in less resplendent costume than other men. They wear no badge of office, do not carry any symbol of authority, nor is their place of residence distinctive. The contexts in which they become noticeable are the settlement of disputes, food exchanges, certain kinds of ritual, and discussions concerning matters affecting the group as a whole. If disputes become so involved that they are seen as between lineages, villages, sibs, or phratries, the "big men" of the units concerned will attempt to arrange a meeting at which most of the members of both groups are present. They do not "conduct" these meetings in any formal sense nor do they sit as arbiters or judges. Rather, they tend to stay in the background while the disputants in the case speak to the points involved; occasionally they will step forward to emphasize a point, clarify an issue, or voice a strong stance. If the issue seems to be reaching an impasse, they frequently resort to long, rambling speeches full of historical illusions, generalities about their own or their group's past achievements, and references to the strength of their group. They are also the men who speak for the group, expressing a consensus informally derived, in instances where the forceful statement of a position rather than appeal to precedent or rule often wins an argument.

The Gururumba engage in food and wealth exchanges at various levels of complexity, but if anything more than an exchange between two individuals is involved, "big men" can be seen playing important parts in various phases of the exchange. In large exchanges, as between tribes, phratries, or sibs, they are often the ones who are instrumental in initiating and organizing the exchange, while in smaller exchanges they oversee the distribution and make set speeches on behalf of the group they represent. The part they play in rituals is much the same. They are not ritual specialists nor are they important figures in all the various types of ritual, but in certain types involving the general well-being of the lineage, village, or sib, they act as organizers and initiators. Finally, in such matters as whether or not the village should be moved, where it should be moved, or whether or not a raid should be carried out against an enemy group, the "big men" are instrumental in formulating opinion and planning action.

It seems inappropriate to describe the role of "big man" in terms of rights and duties. The role is not associated with an office or administrative position, and it is clear that a "big man" is not simply fulfilling obligations when he makes speeches or initiates rituals. Furthermore, the role is not one primarily defined in terms of its relationship to some other role, as in the case of the pair *EvEnE* and *vEnE,* indicating that its content is much more diffuse and general than in roles patterning a specific relationship. The nature of the role becomes clearer if the way people are recruited to it is considered. "Big men" are men of prestige and renown; men whose "names are known," as the Gururumba put it. The characteristics essential to becoming a prestigeful person include physical strength, demonstrated ability as a warrior, heading a lineage, oratorical skill, success in manipulating a rather complex system of economic exchange, an ability to determine and express group consensus, and a forcefulness or assertiveness of character exceeding that of most men. Men with these characteristics, and especially men who actively engage in establishing relationships outside the sib that involve them in economic exchange, gain prestige and become known as *EvEnE nambo.* The power concentrated in this role derives from their ability to attract followers outside the circle of their own immediate kinsmen and the general respect accorded them on the basis of their abilities. Related to this is the fact that the role is not peculiar to any one level of social integration. Rather, the sphere of a "big man's" influence is dependent on the degree of his prestige and it may be limited to his own lineage, his own village, or spread over several villages. It should be emphasized, however, that the sphere of one man's influence is never very large in Gururumba society because there are no institutionalized means for extending it much beyond the sib.

Curers

Certain Gururumba men are referred to as *EvEnE lusuBe. Lusu* denotes a body of magical techniques and practices used for curing illness, predicting the future, attracting lovers, controlling the weather, and ensuring a safe journey. Every adult knows and uses some of these techniques, but some men know especially effective ones and are thought to be more adept at their execution. Although the term *lusuBe* may be applied to a person with special skill in any of these areas, it is most frequently applied to men who cure illnesses.

Once one knows this role exists, it is not difficult to detect men performing it. Curers are always older men in their late forties or fifties. Only a small number of men in the whole upper Asaro valley are regularly asked to act in this capacity and as a result, whenever a curer is called to a village he usually stays two or three days dealing with a number of cases in addition to the one that initially brought him, since it may be some time before he returns to that area. Furthermore, if the illness is at all serious, the cure will involve a number of people in addition to the patient so that it is a highly visible performance.

In very general terms the role of curer involves discovering the cause of illness through divination plus examination of the patient's life history for clues as to potential causes, and carrying out a cure directed at the cause. Determining the nature of the illness is not nearly so important as discovering the cause because the cure is directed at counteracting the cause, which is usually a supernatural agent, rather than symptom relief. Techniques used in diagnosis and cure include divination by smoke, causing the return of body substances extracted by a sorcerer, casting pain out of the body, sucking objects out of the body that have been magically shot into it, and administering various kinds of magical poultice. These techniques are part of the role in the same sense that planting and hunting techniques are part of the male role. The interesting thing from the observer's point of view is that the cures could not possibly be brought about by the techniques themselves. Also, the incidence of actual cures is very small and many of the techniques involve fakery. Sleight-of-hand is frequently used, as when it is made to seem that a magically induced object is sucked from the body. Since a man becomes known as a curer primarily because it is believed that he is highly successful in effecting cures, the ethnographer must also attempt to discover how it is that anyone comes to be seen as successful in a role with failure built into it.

Some of the reasons are not hard to see. First, the Gururumba believe in the effectiveness of the techniques the curer uses. When he finishes working with a patient, the patient is highly disposed to believe he is cured regardless of whether or not there is any manifest change in his condition. Second, this very strong belief may make people feel somewhat better, at least temporarily, after the *lusuBe* has visited them. If malaise returns, it is not usually seen as a failure of the curer but as a new illness. Third, if the curer is confronted with a failure he may explain it as the fault of the patient for not giving him enough information to expose the "real" cause of his trouble. Finally, some of the things the curer deals with are not physical ailments and it is easy to find confirmation for the belief that the *lusuBe* has been successful if one is disposed to do so. For example, a man may feel things are going badly for him; that there is too much in his life of a negative or frustrating sort. He may come to see the untoward events of his life, both important and trivial, as a pattern resulting from malevolent influence of some kind. What the *lusuBe* does for such a person will not alter the circumstances of his life, but it can alter the person's attitude toward future events that will impinge upon him.

There are other factors at work that are not so easily seen because they involve the way a man plays this role so as to make others confident of his abilities. Not all men have the capacity to do this skillfully; consequently, few men are successful in establishing themselves as *lusuBe,* although many try. The factors indicated here are what have been called the techniques of impression management. For example, it is observable that successful *lusuBe* are very careful to reveal to others only those things about themselves tending to substantiate their claim of continued success in curing. They seldom have casual conversations with other people and if they do they limit the topics to a particular case, or long, vivid descriptions of dramatic cures they have effected in the past. They do not speak of their failures nor are they willing to talk casually about the details of their lives not directly related to curing activities. It is interesting in this connection that the well-known curers do not practice in their natal communities and tend to participate less than other men in the regular affairs of their village or kin group. It is also observable that the successful *lusuBe* tend to be selective in the cases they treat. They do not claim to be capable of handling every case and appear to avoid those cases in which the patient is in such poor condition that death seems near: the risk to their reputation is much less in refusing a patient than in failing a patient. Observing these men operate also indicates they have something like a "bedside manner" which instills confidence and trust in others. They are firm, but quietly so. They have a confidently reserved manner contrasting sharply with the flamboyantly assertive manner of "big men." They sympathize with the patient, and people typically go away from their presence expressing admiration for them. Finally, administering a cure is not simply a job done proficiently but has some of the aspects of a performance. They are not spectacles by any means, but they seem carefully staged for dramatic effect. Thus, in the cure where stolen bodily substances are made to return from the sorcerer holding them, the packet in which they eventually appear is conspicuously never touched or even approached by the curer himself. He directs the kinsmen of the patient in its construction and handling, which eliminates any suspicion that the return of the material could have been a plant and contributes to the mystery of its eventual appearance.

To what degree these things are done consciously is beside the point here. The fact is that only those men who have the capacity to manage the situation in these ways become successful curers; therefore observation of these techniques should be included in a description of the role.

Kinsmen

The Gururumba exemplify the kind of society in which many of the named relationships between people are kinship relationships. A large number of Gururumba role names are kin terms and the mere fact of an individual's birth establishes an important series of relationships for him. In Chapter II a set of kin terms was given and an attempt made to identify the dimensions discriminating among them. This section will outline the content of some kinship roles with particular emphasis on that part of the content that structures relationships within the lineage. Using the notion of role in this way helps the ethnographer see identified groups as systems with parts having different functions rather than as a collection of people expressing an identity.

The Gururumba lineage is a patrilineal descent group controlling marriage and certain kinds of property including land. It has an authority structure based partially on age and partially on position in the lineage such that the lineage head is a senior male in the oldest group of lineage siblings still active in public affairs. When the lineage head is superannuated or dies, his younger sibling assumes the headship. Or his eldest son assumes it depending on the age and capabilities of his younger sibling, or if all his siblings have retired from active public life. Looking at the kin terms in this context, we can see that a certain group of them differentiate roles based on differences in sex and seniority within the lineage.

Three pairs of seniority relationships among males within the lineage can be identified: *Ahono-gipE'nE* (father-son), *uBono-naku'nE* (elder brother-younger brother), and *wan ahono-na'Bo* (grandfather-grandson). *Ahono* designates ego's own father and his father's eldest brother, and these men call ego *gipEn'E*. The relationship of both these men to ego is similar in that they make decisions concerning whom ego will marry, what plots of land he will till, and what contributions ego will make to various tasks and events sponsored by the lineage. The relationship is not one-sided since they keep the welfare of ego in mind and contribute food, protection, and valuables to him. *UBono* designates ego's elder brother, father's younger brother, and father's elder brother's son, and these men call ego *naku'nE*. This produces a situation in which each person, even if he is himself an elder brother, has someone whom he calls *uBono* and who calls him *naku'nE*. This is important because the role of *uBono* is one of supportive responsibility toward *naku'nE*. *UBono* organizes the wealth for *naku'nE's* bride price, helps him in the preparation of his first garden, speaks for him in disputes, and contributes heavily to expensive curing ceremonies if *naku'nE* becomes seriously ill. In addition, the *uBono* who is the eldest brother of the most senior group of active siblings is lineage head. His role as lineage head is similar to that of elder brother except that he also acts in the capacity of a group representative. He receives and cares for lineage guests, makes presentations of food and valuables on behalf of the lineage, receives and distributes presentations from outside sources, and is the final authority in the allocation of lineage land. *Wan ahono* (old father) designates father's father, and his male siblings. They call ego *na'Bo* regardless of ego's sex. Life expectancy among the Gururumba is not long and it is rare that ego has personal contact with *wan ahono* beyond his childhood. If the role is activated it is characterized by feeding, friendliness, and even a certain amount of frivolity: *wan ahono* has the authority of age but exercises very little control over *na'Bo* in economic or other terms.

Thinking back to the earlier attempt to formulate the major dimensions that produce the various categories of kinship, we can see that terms that appeared to differentiate kinsmen on the basis of relative age or generation are better understood now as differentiating them on the basis of seniority within the lineage. The men called *ahono* are ego's own father and the head of ego's patrilineage; those called *uBono* are ego's elder brother and men who are immediately potential successors to lineage headship; those called *naku'nE* are ego's younger brother and men who would succeed to lineage headship only after ego; those called *gipE'nE* and *na'Bo* are ego's son and grandson plus the descendents of other lineage mates too young to consider as bearers of authority. This interpretation can be supported by pointing out that the lineage is the unit within which these terms are most consistently used, even to the exclusion of personal names. If this interpretation is accepted, the further implication is that the use of these terms to address a person outside the lineage is an extension of the term in the sense that the person so addressed does not habitually play the full role designated by the term but is being asked to enact a part of it temporarily. Thus, as noted in Chapter III, sib mates who are not also lineage mates may be addressed by these terms, and observation indicates this is usually done either as a matter of respect for advanced age or as a prelude to asking a favor of some kind. Such extended usage emphasizes the role's nurtural and helpful rather than authoritarian aspect—a point neatly exemplified when an old man will approach a young sib mate, call him father, and ask for tobacco, food, or a small favor.

Another set of roles in some respects parallels those between male members of a lineage but is not related so directly to the lineage structure. This comprises the roles of *iJEno, atEno aru'nE,* and *arunE*. The persons to whom these terms are primarily applied are ego's mother, the wives of ego's lineage mates, ego's female siblings, ego's daughters, and the daughters of ego's lineage mates. In other words, some terms applied to females are connected to the lineage both consanguineally and affinally. Furthermore, because most women leave their natal lineage at marriage, some terms refer to some women resident both in ego's lineage and in other lineages. It is therefore understandable that although these roles structure authority with reference to ego according to relative age, it is authority derived from greater age alone rather than from the combination of greater age and seniority in the lineage.

IJEno and *atEno* are persons ego can look to for protection, food, and hospitality. The content of these roles varies importantly according to the exact genealogical link between ego and alter, ego's age, and ego's sex. For the sake of simplicity and consistency in this brief discussion, a male ego will be assumed throughout. *IJEno* includes ego's own mother, mother's elder sister, father's elder sister, and the wives of senior lineage mates. When ego is an infant and young child, his own mother behaves toward him in a nurtural, protective, and supportive manner. The Gururumba do not see the role as "disciplinarian" or "trainer," and mothers seldom attempt to impose any kind of strict regimen or physical punishment on ego. From about the age of seven or eight, boys begin to associate more and more with other boys of approximately their own age. It is at this point that individuals other than ego's own mother begin playing the role of *iJEno* in an important degree. As ego grows older, *iJEno* becomes a term applied to several women beyond his immediate family who have approximately the same capacity to effect his life.

AtEno includes ego's own elder sister and the sisters and wives of lineage mates junior to ego. *AtEno,* especially as elder sister, is a very important figure to ego, and interesting because of the "warmth" characterizing the role. Elder sister cares for younger brother as a child, carrying him on her back, playing with him, and sharing food with him. Close emotional attachments are frequent between individuals so related, and when elder sister is sent away in marriage it frequently produces trauma for younger brother. In fact, the situation has become institutionalized in the form of a stick fight that takes place just before the girl is handed over to her husband's lineage between all the young people in a village and all the adults led by the girl's younger brother. He attempts to keep his sister from being sent away, but after vigorous effort is always defeated. The character of the relationship is also depicted in stories involving elder sister and younger brother as the main characters. These stories are quite poignant, as they are in the form of tragedies showing one of the pair vainly trying to protect the other against harm. For example, one tells of an elder sister who discovers her father has eaten her mother while the two of them were out gathering vines. She knows he will eat younger brother and herself next, so in the night she carries younger brother away, setting fire to the house as she leaves to prevent father from following by burning him to death. All seems well as she searches for a new home, but she falls into the clutches of a two-headed witch and must stand by helplessly as the witch eats younger brother finger by finger, arm by arm, and leg by leg. Her own escape is only accomplished by promising to marry a sorcerer who destroys the witch through his superior powers.

Ego's relationship to *aru'nE* and *arunE* is somewhat different. The first term refers to his own younger sister and the daughters of lineage mates junior to him, the second term to his own daughters. He is, respectively, "elder brother" and "father" to them and as such exercises control over them particularly concerning their marriage. A man's younger sister is less under his control in this respect than his own daughter and again it is interesting that tales depict a relationship of greater affective attachment between the sibling pair than between the filial pair. In tales featuring this sibling pair, for example, elder brother is frequently depicted as leading younger sister through all the ceremonies of marriage, and while he protects her from danger during this time there comes a point at which he must abandon her to the care of her spouse's lineage. At this juncture disaster overwhelms her in such forms as cannibalistic in-laws or demonic nature spirits. After marriage both *aru'nE* and *arunE* provide important links between ego and the natal members of alien villages, and they are expected to extend hospitality and food to ego should he come to the village where they are resident. There will also be women in these villages ego calls *atEno,* but since ego had no hand in arranging the marriages of these women his closest contact with the natal members of an alien village will be through *aru'nE* and *arunE.*

Each of the roles discussed has many contexts of action outside the lineage itself and a more comprehensive description would characterize the patterned actions appropriate to those contexts. By focusing on the single context of the lineage, and its authority structure, a number of roles can be compared with one another against a common background.

5

The Flow of Objects

"Give Me!" "Take!"

I
N THE TWO preceding chapters we have tried to see order in Gururumba life
by examining the way behavior is patterned in social groups and social
roles. The human scene thus is seen as a system of parts standing in ordered
relationships to one another. Beyond the question of what the parts are, this
particular point of view suggests many others, such as how the parts maintain
their identity and how the system achieves integration. Such highly abstract
questions are major analytic rather than empirical objectives, but they are approached at the empirical or ethnographic level by observation of various aspects of the interaction between individuals playing certain roles and representing certain groups. For example, the ethnographer may observe interaction in
an attempt to see how the learning of values or norms takes place, how power
is wielded, or how groups maintain their boundaries. In this chapter the focus
will be on a series of observations of the flow of objects between individuals and
groups and an attempt to discern the social functions of this flow.

Gift Exchange in the Gururumba Setting

Cultures vary considerably in the emphasis placed on the accumulation
and exchange of food, utilitarian objects, or items of value. Only a little ac-
quaintance with the Gururumba shows they are very much concerned with these
matters. A few weeks living with them convinces the outsider they are "thing-
oriented," that they have an overriding concern with material objects. As re-
counted in Chapter I, on our arrival in the village of Miruma it became apparent that the people were not so much interested in us as in our possessions, and
when their interest did turn to us it was initially because we might provide links
to the "red man's" world of material goods.

Other observations tend to substantiate this impression. In the first instance, Gururumba are noticeably fond of "taking inventory." Men will fre-

51

quently sit down with their stocks of shells, feathers, decorative armbands, necklaces, and pieces of Australian money to count and fondle them. This is sometimes done as a genuine stocktaking prior to payment of a debt or making a loan, but it is also done simply for the pleasure it gives. They do not have an elaborate counting system as do other peoples in New Guinea (indeed it becomes cumbersome above ten and almost impossible above twenty), but they do keep track of numbers of items by bundling sticks together, each stick representing one item and each bundle a class of items. Next, the most frequent topic of conversation among the adult men in a village concerns the number and size of pigs, taro patches, banana plantations, sugar cane stands, and yam patches. How many piglets of each sex in a new litter, how fat a man's sow, how many pigs are owed a man, how tall his sugar cane, how numerous his bunches of bananas, how gigantic his yams, and how abundant his gardens are matters the Gururumba never tire or hearing or talking about. Men carry little sticks with them marked so as to demonstrate the thickness of fat on their sows or the length of tusk on their boars, and every man's house has a rack outside for displaying the jaws of all pigs given the members of that house for many years past.

Finally, the impression of concern with objects comes from what might be called the tenor of daily life. There is a great deal of banter between people, both young and old, centered around such small favors as giving another a bite of sweet potato, letting someone have a puff on your cigarette, giving someone a small piece of dried banana leaf in which to roll a cigarette, breaking off a section of sugar cane for another person, or lending another your digging stick or shovel. Two things impress the outsider about this behavior: its frequency and the manner in which it occurs. Sit with a small group of Gururumba for half an hour and you will hear dozens of such requests made; watch a group of children and you will see they amuse themselves by "pestering" one another for bits of rubbish or other inconsequential objects in a child's version of the adult pattern. To call these actions "requests" is a misnomer for they are made in the form of demands. Thus, when one man asks another for tobacco he will probably do so by using a verbal form best translated into English as "Give me!" If the potential giver refuses or claims he has no tobacco, the person making the demand will frequently accuse him of lying and may go so far as to search his person in an attempt to ferret out the supposedly hidden item. If the giver relinquishes the item in question, it is usually done with a shouted, "Take!" It must be emphasized that this is usual behavior not only between persons in a superordinate-subordinate relationship, but among village mates; it is the most common mode of social intercourse. This demandlike behavior is not the only mode in which things are solicited from other people. An older person may take on the demeanor of a child, or a young man that of an *EvEnE nambo* as a prelude to asking for something; the multiplicity of the forms contributes to the impression that the Gururumba are "thing-oriented."

The Gururumba might more accurately be characterized as "exchange-oriented," however, for they appear more concerned with controlling the flow of objects than with the objects themselves. There are three sets of observations barring on this statement. First, it is observable that public, formalized gift exchange occurs frequently. These occasions involve from as few as two to as many as a thousand or more people, the participants being divided into a host group and a guest group. In very general terms, one side is obligated to the other in some way, and the point of the exchange is to discharge the obligation through presentation of food and wealth objects. Exchange by barter or purchase is another type and the Gururumba themselves refer to it by a different term. Accurate records were kept on the exchange activities in the village of Miruma for a period of fifty weeks. In that period there were 110 occasions in which the forty-five or so adult males of the village were involved in exchanges of this type, averaging more than two per week.

Second, there is a noticeable elaboration and institutionalization of instances when obligation can be incurred and discharged through gift exchange. Many of these are built around points in the individual's life history and involve exchanges among ego's father's kinsmen and ego's mother's kinsmen, among people related affinely through ego, or among ego's parents and other members of the lineage and ward. Some of these occasions are birth, naming, walking, the assumption of hair ornaments by prepubescent girls, nose-piercing for boys, a boy's first productive hunt, the onset of menstruation, male initiation, the rejection of a girl's marriage offer to a boy of her choice, betrothal, the passage of a betrothed girl's first month in her new village, the planting of a betrothed girl's first garden, the presentation of first food by a wife to her husband, any pregnancy, the first crop from any new garden, the successful conduct of a trading expedition, preparation for death, and death itself.

Most of these occasions do not simply provide the basis for a single exchange between the parties concerned, but involve a whole complex of exchanges. Male initiation, for example, consists of a series of rituals and taboo periods, each marked by an exchange, occurring over a ten- to twelve-month period. In addition to exchanges of this type others are related to the pattern of reciprocity between villagers and lineage mates. People within these groups are expected to aid in a variety of tasks such as house building, carrying out an exchange, clearing land for a garden, or cutting and carrying long poles from the forest to prop up sugar cane. The Gururumba say no compensation is expected for this kind of help and that helping others ensures help for yourself when needed. However, help of this kind is always followed by an exchange in which the person receiving help feeds the helpers and presents them with small gifts such as salt or sugar cane. In other words, instances of reciprocity are made into occasions for exchange.

Finally, there are exchanges involving groups of large size such as the village, the sib, and the phratry. Some of these repay another group for helping in warfare against an enemy. Others repay a group for providing protection and shelter for a vanquished people who have been driven from their land by an enemy. Some are exchanges based on the reestablishment of peace between two groups who have seriously disputed with one another. The largest exchanges in terms of numbers of people involved and amount of goods distributed have no single reason for their occurrence but are built around the specific obligation existing between a large number of individuals. These are held at fairly regular intervals between groups on good terms with one another whenever one group considers its resources are sufficient to the task. In all these instances the main exchange is followed by a smaller exchange given by the guest group in recognition of their host's efforts.

Third, it is clear from the form that these exchanges take and the speeches made during their course that it is the activity of exchange itself that is important to the Gururumba rather than a materialistic interest in things. The exchanges vary somewhat in form, depending on the ocassion and the number of people involved, but an element common to all of them is the food and wealth display. Whatever is being presented in an exchange, no matter how large or small the amount, is always displayed prior to presentation in a symmetrically arranged pile. In a small exchange such a pile might consist of a base made by arranging bundles of cut pieces of sugar cane arranged in a hollow square, a filling for the square consisting of several layers of different kinds of sweet potatoes and yams, and on top a bunch of bananas decorated with multicolored leaves. The whole pile might only measure three or four feet along each side and be intended for half a dozen recipients. At the other extreme are displays made by erecting a large square tower some ten to fifteen feet along the sides of the base and rising twenty-five or more feet into the air. This tower provides a framework for a huge pile of food and wealth objects, such as shells or pieces of cloth, whose combined weight would be several tons. Such a display would be distributed among three to four hundred people. It takes a great deal of planning, work, and coordination of effort to erect one of these displays, even a small one, and the men who put them together are proud of their accomplishment. The displays are not simply of accumulated riches; they are displays of the capacity to be productive and energetic. This is explicitly recognized in the speeches made at the time the displays are presented. Speakers for the host group extol the strength and vitality of the group or individual acting as host, and speakers for the guest group also recognize their proficiency.

These observations all indicate that gift exchange is an elaborately developed institution among the Gururumba and functions as an important medium for the expression of social relations.

Gift Exchange and the Ordering of Daily Affairs

From the information in the preceding section it is clear that participation in exchange activities is a focal point of Gururumba life. Observation also indicates that daily affairs, especially for adult males, are importantly patterned by anticipated involvement in gift exchanges. This is true with respect to both food-producing and social activities.

Gururumba food-producing technology is such that every able-bodied adult works in the direct production of food. However, pig raising, gardening, and land management are geared to more than producing the necessities of daily subsistence. This can be most easily seen in the utilization and raising of pigs. Pigs are never killed only to provide meat for daily consumption. A gift of pork, or of a live pig, is the most important item a person can give in a food presentation, and pigs are saved for such occasions. Thus, although a pig may sometimes be killed because it has become sick or is about to die, its meat is not simply eaten by the owners; some reason is found for turning the untimely death into a food presentation. This feeling that pork is too valuable to waste on daily consumption is so strong that it effects the pattern of protein consumption. Pork is the major source of animal protein for the Gururumba, who either get only a few ounces of meat per week or get so much in a short time that they can hardly consume it. More than this, however, the manner in which a man tends his pigs clearly shows that he is not thinking of them as a food resource but as an exchange resource. The pig herds are not kept at an approximately constant size by regular slaughtering to provide a supply of meat, but vary cyclically with the demands of exchange activity. In the short run the size of a herd fluctuates with the small-scale and frequent demands associated with life-cycle events or the meeting of other interpersonal obligations. In the long run the size of a herd increases steadily through a five- to seven-year period. At that time almost all pigs will be killed for a very large exchange called the *idzi namo,* or pig festival, leaving only enough to reseed the herd. Also, there is an interesting pattern of farming out mature pigs. Each man has some pigs that other men keep for him. They receive a portion of each litter for their efforts, and the owner, who keeps the matter secret, is protected from excessive demands being made on him because the exact number of his pigs is not known. It is also a convenient way for a man to keep more pigs than his land can support.

Gardening activities follow much the same pattern. It was mentioned earlier that although both men and women work in the gardens, they tend different crops. The crops tended by the men, such as bananas, sugar cane, or taro, are raised primarily for use in exchange activities, while the crops raised by women are the staples of daily fare. The Gururumba recognize this distinction by applying different names to these two classes of food. The prestige foods, as we will refer to the crops raised by men, are occasionally eaten as part of the regular diet. This is especially true of sugar cane, which is plentiful, but except for this the eating of prestige crops is much like the eating of a sick pig—it is done to avoid waste and may itself be the impetus for a small-scale exchange. It is also observable that the planting, tending, and harvesting of prestige crops is attended by more concern and ceremony than is evident for ordinary crops. For example, sugar cane is allowed to grow fifteen to twenty feet tall, but because of its great weight and slender stalk, cane this tall would fall over unless supported by a prop. The production of these props has been elaborated into a ceremonial occasion by the Gururumba. Instead of using bamboo poles or young saplings for the props, both of which are readily available, groups of men who have promised someone they will make his props for him go into the forest and cut down large trees several feet in diameter from which they laboriously split off slabs twenty feet or more in length. These are eventually cut down to the appropriate shape, decorated, and presented as a group to the man being helped who then uses the occasion for a food presentation. It might also be noted that there is more magic associated with the growing of these crops than with others.

Land management includes two kinds of activity. One consists of the actions a man takes to utilize the land he has for his particular needs, and the other the actions he takes to safeguard or expand his claim to land. Participation in exchange affects both these kinds of activity. When a Gururumba is deciding what to plant, where and when, he keeps in mind that his gardens must supply both his daily needs and his exchange needs. As a result he has several gardens planted with everyday crops, each in a different stage of growth and he also has a series of plots, each with one or two kinds of prestige crops. The first kind of garden tends to be large and in areas with greatly differing soil conditions. The second is smaller and in areas where conditions are best for growing the particular crop to which it is devoted. It is frequently at the side or edge of a garden of the first type. A third kind of garden is much like the first in that it has a variety of crops within it, but it is smaller in size and is planted to provide for a particular anticipated exchange rather than for daily use. A man knows that his daughter's marriage, his son's initiation, or the pig festival will be coming and in preparation he may plant a garden a year or more in advance. Such a garden will be largely stripped when the event is at hand and allowed to return to fallow more quickly than usual. Given the system of crop rotation used by the Gururumba and the special needs created by the exchange system, it is incumbent on a man that he keep careful track of what state his various gardens are in so he can plan his land needs. This is especially true for prestige crops requiring special growing conditions. The Gururumba seem to have enough land to meet their basic needs, but there is not always enough land just right for taro or just right for bananas. Because of this a man must be careful that others do not usurp his claim to these special plots, and at the same time he must actively seek to establish claim to additional plots of this sort if he wishes to expand his exchange activities. Most court cases concerning land are disputes over these special plots associated most directly with exchange activity.

The manner in which concern with exchange activities structures daily affairs can also be seen in social activities on either an individual or group level. This is most evident when considering relations between individuals from different villages, sibs, or phratries, because the planning and execution of exchanges is the major basis on which individuals outside the village come together and interact. A Gururumba village is a relatively closed unit; one does not see people in it who are strangers or whose links with the village are unknown to most of its members. Furthermore, people do not simply go into a village other than their own, even if they are known there, unless they have been invited or unless they have come to discuss a particular matter: sight-seeing and casual visiting are patterns only now becoming known to the Gururumba through the changes wrought by European contact. Individuals from different villages come together in the first instance because they want to arrange, carry out, or argue about exchanges. The relationships between ego and those kinsmen living outside his own village, for example, are ordered in large part by the obligations existing between them concerning exchanges. Some of these relationships are very specific with respect to the occasions when participation in exchange activity is expected, but others are more diffuse so that it is primarily a matter of individual choice how deeply the kinsmen become involved. Thus, the kinsman called *omono* (mother's brother) is expected to be the chief mourner outside the nuclear family if ego dies while a child. On hearing of ego's death, *omono* appears in the village with a group of his own lineage mates, wails loudly, and attacks the deceased person's lineage for not watching after his sister's son more closely. He is calmed, presented with food and wealth in recognition of his grief, and in turn presents a live pig to the deceased's family as an expression of sympathy for the bereaved. This is only one of the many specific obligations that exist between *omono* and ego's kinsmen bringing them together from time to time. An example of a relationship with more diffuse exchange obligations is that between ego and his brother-in-law. Men so related have the right to ask one another for aid in arranging exchanges, particularly as this might involve loaning pigs, shells, feather pieces of Australian money, or work in preparing a garden. Some men so related become indebted to one another or freely give of their time and effort to arrange a food presentation, but others do not. Whether or not this happens is related to factors quite outside the nature of the relationship itself, such as age differences, spatial contiguity, and personal liking. The point is that if the relationship is activated at all, it will find its most meaningful expression in exchange-related activities.

Interpersonal relations outside the village are so much structured by exchange activities that the Gururumba tend to think of them primarily in terms of exchange potential. This is especially true of men who are or who are trying to become "big men." Thus, there are several young girls to whom a man applies the term "daughter." Some are his real daughters and some are classificatory daughters. A "big man" will actively become involved in arranging the marriages of these girls and will attempt to find husbands for them in a wide variety of sibs rather than marrying them all into a single sib. The reasoning behind this is that a marriage is the starting point for a whole series of kin ties between the members of the bride's sib and the groom's sib, and each of these ties is the focal point for exchange activity. By marrying daughters into several sibs, the potential number of exchanges one can engage in is increased. There are a variety of reasons for this, but one of the most important is that it creates ties with a larger number of individuals of any particular kin class and therefore avoids reduplication of exchange activity. The Gururumba also point out that if all one's daughters are married into a single sib and relations with that sib break down, the number of exchange relationships a man has will be drastically instead of minimally reduced, as they would be if his affinal ties were scattered among several sibs.

The structuring of affairs through exchange is also apparent at the group level. Participating as a unit in some kind of exchange is part of what all Gururumba social groups do. The nuclear family gardens together and lives together—at least some of the time; it also comprises a unit in one kind of exchange relationship unique to the nuclear family. This relationship exists between the family and a nature spirit. The spirit dwells in a miniature house built in one of the family's gardens, and in return for food presented by the family as a unit, it helps tend the gardens or watches after the pigs. The lineage acts as a unit in the complex of exchanges centering around first menstruation and around the harvesting of the first crop from the new garden of one of its members. The village becomes a unit in funeral ceremonies especially when an important man has died: it receives, feeds, and presents gifts to guest mourners. The sib is the main unit in the pig festival, the most complex exchange activity of all. Phratries and tribes seldom act as hosts in an exchange activity, but they occasionally appear as units in the role of guest. All the tribes in the upper Asaro valley never act together as a cohesive unit, but analytically they can be seen as a unit because any tribe within the area carries on more exchanges with tribes in the same area than with tribes outside the area.

The observations listed in this section provide a kind of documentation for the point that much of what goes on in daily affairs among the Gururumba is ordered and arranged in terms of exchange activities. In addition to noting that gift exchange is something the Gururumba do, the ethnologist can also see gift exchange as "doing something" for Gururumba society: i.e., it can be viewed analytically in terms of its social functions.

Gift Exchange and Gururumba Society

Preceding discussions of the various levels of social integration among the Gururumba have shown that social groups above the level of the patrilineage represent something more than patrilineal descent groups. The sib, for example, does not use patrilineal descent as the only principle of recruitment nor is authority within the sib structured by the descent relationships of its members. Furthermore, the relationship between lineage, ward, village, sib, phratry, and tribe does not correspond to a series of increasingly inclusive descent groups. To understand the internal integration of any one of these groups, or the integration of all of them into a single system, it is therefore necessary to go beyond descent to locate integrative mechanisms; gift exchange can be viewed as one such mechanism.

In looking for the sources of integration of the ward, for example, it is noted that a ward consists of all the lineages in a village whose initiated males are identified with a single men's house. It is true that most of the lineages in a ward claim dimly known patrilineal links with one another, but some lineages trace connection to the ward through affinal ties while others have no known kin ties or only very remote and tangential matrilineal ties. Furthermore, the members of a ward think of themselves as a group held together not so much by one kind of genealogical tie as by ties of reciprocity among themselves and allegiance to a "big man." The focal point of a ward is not an ancestral figure located in the past, but a prestigeful figure located in the present, and the sources of integration are much more in the power structure than in the kinship structure. Power, it will be remembered, comes largely from renown gained in gift exchange.

The Uphill ward in the village of Miruma can be taken as a concrete example of what is meant here. This ward consists of five resident lineages. The composition of each lineage, described in terms of married "couples" without reference to polygamous unions, is as follows:

L 1—eight married couples including three in which the females are L 1 daughters, and one couple in which the male is a collateral relative of the husband of an L 1 daughter.

L 2—eight married couples including one couple in which the male is a lineal of an L 2 wife.

L 3—eleven married couples including one couple in which the male is a lineal relative of an L 3 daughter, and four couples in which the males are collateral relatives of L 3 wives.

L 4—one couple of immigrant Gende.

L 5—one couple of immigrant Chimbu.

It can be seen that twelve of the twenty-nine couples in this ward, or 41 percent of its couples, are connected to the ward by nonpatrilineal ties. In addition, the first three lineages, which all have a core of patrilineally related males, only suppose they are related to one another and cannot actually trace clear genealogical links. At the time of the field study, the most prominent man in the Uphill ward was LuBiso, the oldest male in L 1. The integration of this ward cannot be understood without understanding his position in it.

It is usually the case that the lineage of a "big man" like LuBiso is the largest in the ward, but as the preceding tabulation indicates, this is not true of L 1 and there is evidence that a shift in the locus of power was taking place in this ward at the time of the field study. However, LuBiso was still in fact the most prominent man in the ward. He had twelve wives during his life, four of whom were still with him, and the ties established with other groups through these unions and their offspring gave him a social field in which to operate of greater extent than anyone else in the ward. He was a warrior of note and when walking from one village to another frequently took the occasion to recount stories of fights he participated in at points along the route, a convenient technique for reminding others of his past achievements. His name was well known not only in the Asaro valley but in neighboring areas as well. In fact, the families from Gende and Chimbu settled in Miruma because of admiration and personal liking for LuBiso. The next village to the north of Miruma is inhabited entirely by Chimbu who originally came into the valley as battle allies of LuBiso's sib but were so impressed with him that they decided to leave the Chimbu valley and settle near his land.

LuBiso is thought of as having the good name and welfare of the whole group in mind when he acts and as being willing to make sacrifices for the group. A striking example of this attitude toward him can be seen in a story told by several people independently concerning the introduction of a new ritual item by LuBiso. The peoples to the west of the Gururumba in the Chimbu and Wahgi valleys wear a distinctive wig made by matting human hair in a small, rigid, curtain-shaped bamboo framework which is tied to the back of the head and hung to the shoulders. These wigs are worn during the pig festival and are thought to induce fertility and growth in pigs and gardens. LuBiso is said to have deliberately set out for Chimbu when a young man to learn the making and ritual manipulation of these wigs so that men of his sib could wear them in an upcoming pig festival. This was not only to create a sensation among those observing the dance, because of its novelty, but also to contribute magically to the strength of the group. The wigs are dangerous, however, if not handled correctly and he made himself quite sick several times before learning the proper means of manipulating them. Regardless of the facts of the actual introduction of this cultural item to the Gururumba, people believe the story and use it to illustrate the qualities they admire in LuBiso. LuBiso also has the kind of personality admired in a "big man," being somewhat more forceful and assertive than most men. On several occasions he dismissed minor claims made against him for damages by his pigs or dogs simply by announcing loudly that he did not have time to consider such trivial matters. There would be reaction against LuBiso if he became truly despotic, but in relatively unimportant matters of this sort his forcefulness is taken as the sign of a strong, vigorous personality.

All these factors combine to make LuBiso the kind of man who attracts followers. His extensive social contacts are avenues other men can utilize in establishing their own exchange relationships, and the vigor of his own exchange activity assures participation in many food distributions. Attracting followers is only part of what makes LuBiso the focal point of the ward, however. Examination of his activities shows that he binds people to him economically. His economic resources are greater than anyone else's in Miruma and he uses them to support the exchange activities of others. When one man repays the support given, LuBiso uses the income to support someone else or to expand his own resources so that an even wider group can become the recipients of his help. People are tied to him by debt, by dependence on him as a source of resources and as a source of contacts. It is as if LuBiso were making an investment of material wealth through his exchange activities in which the profit was prestige rather than more material wealth. Remembering that prestige is power and that the ward's power structure is based on prestige, one can begin to understand the importance of gift exchange in holding this group together.

Rather similar factors operate to hold the village and sib together. A village has more than one ward, but the ward of the most prominent man is the focal point of the village. Similarly, one of the villages in a sib will be considered as having within it a "big man" of greater prominence than other "big men" in the sib and greater control over exchange activities will be concentrated in that village than in others. As in the ward, the power structure in the sib corresponds to the prestige structure rather than the genealogical structure. The "big men" in a sib are heads of lineages, but their authority derives from their effectiveness in exchange activities rather than from an ethic of kinship.

Furthermore, the members of a sib see their interrelationship as coparticipants in exchange activity rather than as segments of a familistic unit. Sib mates are meaningful to one another because they jointly constitute a unit that can effectively prepare for and carry out the pig festival and other kinds of large-scale exchanges demonstrating the strength and vitality of the group to outsiders. Engaging in exchange is not only a matter of discharging obligations, it is also a means of expressing some of the most important values in Gururumba culture. These values concern the ability of a man or a group to be strong, to grow abundant crops, to raise a defense against attackers, to be assertive, and to produce healthy, vital children. One seeks many obligations to discharge as a means of demonstrating these abilities; it is in the grand manner. Far from being just a kind of interesting economic game for the Gururumba, engaging in exchange is a mode of self-expression on the individual level and a means of achieving identity on the group level.

Just as exchange can be seen as relating to the integration of social units within Gururumba society, it can also be seen as relating to the integration of the total social system. Several points might be discussed here, but only one will be mentioned. Every society has some institutionalized means for distributing food and resources among its members, and such a distributive network connects certain of the segments of a society with one another. In societies like the Gururumba where there is no market economy gift exchange constitutes the distributive network, and the boundaries of the society are largely defined by the limits of exchange activity. It is interesting to note that the Gururumba do not think of trade except in the context of social relationships involving exchange obligations. That is, trading partners barter with one another, but only rarely do people barter who are not already linked to one another through gift exchange. As the Gururumba put it, if a man wants to barter for the oil-bearing pandanus nuts found in the Gende area, he must first activate an affinal tie or a distant matrilineal tie by meeting the exchange obligations implied in these links to create a "road" leading to a trade partner. Incidentally, several kinds of quasi kin ties can be established for the same purpose if no direct links exist. Thus, the distributive network not only operates through exchange activities, but the existence of relationships involving exchange establishes further ties accomplishing the flow of resources in terms other than reciprocal gift exchange.

6

Ritual and Social Structure

"Women cannot see the flutes."

THE GURURUMBA IDENTIFY a number of entities and forces in the world that we would label supernatural and have institutionalized means for dealing with them that we would call ritual. A stranger among the Gururumba can observe the rituals and learn of the entities without much difficulty. What he learns from observation and conversation concerns the form of the rituals and their immediate aim, or the names of entities and their major attributes. This knowledge may seem superficial, comprising a set of curious and disparate items, because the Gururumba are not given to talking about them as objects of contemplation nor, therefore, the assumptions on which such matters are based or in what way they constitute a system. The ethnologist attempts to consider these questions by arranging the items of ritual and belief he collects to reveal their relationship to other institutionalized systems, their thematic connections with one another, or the view of man and nature they imply. In this chapter, and the next two, I will describe parts of Gururumba supernaturalism and ritual in these three kinds of arrangement. The present chapter aims at arranging a series of rituals according to the social groups characteristically carrying them out so as to suggest possible relationships between ritual and social structure.

Nature Spirits and the Family

When walking with the Gururumba outside their villages or gardens, or especially through unfamiliar territory, one notices that they are quite cautious. They seldom stray from the clearly marked paths and manifest little interest in exploring the countryside. This is partly because they still retain some fear of being ambushed, partly because they want to avoid straying onto someone else's property, and partly because they fear being attacked by nature spirits. There is no generic name for these spirits, but there are two varieties of them:

nokondisi, which live in the upland forest zone, and *gwomai,* which inhabit the clumps of tall reeds and riverbanks of the lowlands. Aside from this difference in location there seem to be no other differences between the two kinds of spirits. Neither of them is easily seen because they are said to be like smoke or mist, meaning they are physically present but transparent. There are quite definite notions concerning their physical characteristics, however. They are male, and occur in a number of fantastic semihuman forms such as half-men, bats with human heads, or with long hair covering their bodies. They may also change from one form to another even including the fully human form. Certain physical signs are taken as indicating their presence in an area, such as a certain kind of fecal material and pieces of half-eaten food with the marks of tiny teeth on them.

By looking over all the events whose cause has been attributed to nature spirits, a summative statement can be formulated concerning their behavioral characteristics. First, they have lusty sexual appetites, but since there are no female nature spirits they satisfy themselves with human females. The birth of twins, considered abnormal by the Gururumba, is attributed to such a relationship. Second, nature spirits have proprietary interests. Each spirit has its own dwelling place—a certain clump of reeds, a particular configuration of boulders along the river, or the exposed roots of some tree. Anyone wandering into one of these sanctuaries is attacked by the spirit which may cause him illness or even death. The Gururumba do not conceive such attacks as motivated by maliciousness but only by the spirit's desire to defend its property against invasion. Third, ritual contact with a nature spirit can bring about good health and can increase a person's strength and productivity. Finally, nature spirits are motivated by ideals of reciprocity. One can enter into a relationship with a nature spirit that resembles a contractual agreement. Every adult male with a family has a small fenced enclosure called a *ropo'ne* in one of his gardens. Inside the fence is a dome-shaped hut about two feet in diameter with an entryway and a miniature earth oven in front. This is the dwelling place of a nature spirit with which a man has entered into a reciprocal agreement. The man provides the spirit with a house, food from each of the gift exchanges he initiates, and information about his gardening activities and the disposition of his pig herd. In return the spirit takes a proprietary interest in the man's gardens and pigs. It protects the gardens against theft and rides herd on the pigs when they are not under human supervision. It may even "doctor" the pigs if they are ill or receive an injury.

The ritual itself is quite simple. Small amounts of food are prepared and placed in the earth oven. Meat is always presented: if a pig has recently been killed cooked pieces of its liver and heart will be offered, otherwise, rats and mice. As water is being poured over the hot stones in the bottom of the cooking hole to produce the steam that cooks the food, all the family members gather in close and speak to the spirit. After the food is cooked it is eaten by the family except for a very small portion placed in the spirit house. There are two reasons for performing the ritual, and what is said in the speeches depends on which reason is involved. Each time a man kills one of his pigs the ritual is performed to compensate the spirit for having watched after that pig and to assuage the anger of the spirit at the killing of one of "his" pigs. The ritual may also be performed to cure illness caused either by the spirit or by some unknown agent. In the former case the cure consists of placating an angry spirit which is attacking a person and making him ill for some "breach of contract," and in the latter case the cure consists of putting an ill person in physical contact with the strong, vital, qualities of the spirit in order to restore those qualities to the patient. In fact, whenever a ritual is performed at the *ropo'ne,* for whatever reason, it is thought to increase the vital energies of those involved.

Presentation of food to a nature spirit is a ritual exclusive to the nuclear family. A man and his wife, or wives, plus their unmarried children are the only ones who participate, and a man will not allow even his own brother or father into the *ropo'ne* enclosure. Furthermore, it is the only ritual in which the family acts as a unit, and in which the unity of the family is stressed. One of the interesting things about the form of this ritual is the fact that men and women perform the same actions in it: both pour water into the earth oven, both help prepare the food, and both speak with the spirit. In all other rituals they either perform different actions or do not participate in the same rite thus emphasizing their complementarity and separateness. The family, it will be remembered, is residentially segregated much of the time and the task patterns of its members are sharply differentiated by the sexual division of labor. Nonetheless, the family is the basic producing unit in Gururumba society, and the ritual at the *ropo'ne* brings the family together to augment and maintain their productive capacity.

Rituals of the Lineage

There is no single ritual characteristic of the lineage as there is of the family, and some of the rituals performed by the lineage may, on occasion, be performed in a broader social context. These extensions can justifiably be viewed as special circumstances, however, in the sense that rituals come to be occasions for gift exchange. With this proviso in mind, one class of rituals is usually performed by a lineage, namely, the life-crisis rites.

Life-crisis rites occur at points in an individual's life when some significant change is thought to be taking place in his social position. Among the Gururumba there are many such points, mostly concentrated in childhood and early adulthood, some of which were noted in the last chapter in connotation with various occasions for gift exchange. Male initiation, which occurs around the time of puberty, is the only one that is not primarily a lineage ritual. There is not space here to describe all these rituals even briefly, so only the series centering around birth and a few other life-crisis rites will be discussed.

Actual birth is attended by only a few older women of the village who aid the mother in delivery. No males, including the father, may enter the house during birth because it would pollute them. The infant and its mother remain in the house for at least five days. Many visitors come and go during this period of isolation because birth is an exciting and eagerly awaited event, but no male may yet enter since it is thought that the fluids of birth, which have only been recently cleared away, might cause them illness or weaken their physical powers. Food and firewood are brought by lineage mates to the mother and father, for both of them suspend all gardening and collecting activities during this period. The mother is not yet able to return to her work after the ordeal of birth and the father abstains from labor for the sake of his child. It is felt that such actions as splitting wood, chopping trees, or pounding of any kind might break the bones of the child.

On the second or third day after birth, a naming ceremony is held. This is an affair of the lineage and requires the killing of at least one pig. The pig belongs to the father, but he does not kill it himself to avoid harming his child. All those attending the naming ceremony gather outside the house where the mother and child are secluded and begin filling an earth oven. It is an easy, pleasant occasion, but there is great concern for the fragile infant inside the house. People are cautioned not to talk loudly in order that the child may not be disturbed; wood for the fire is split at a distance from the house because of the noise; the pig is muzzled when it is killed to prevent its squeals from being heard in the house. All males must be cautious in their actions as they go about the business of building fires and preparing food lest they harm the child with the forcefulness of their actions. Even such a seemingly innocuous act as dropping nuts into a dish must be done with care.

If the mother is having difficulty with lactation, this is remedied by a little ritual performed by the older men of the lineage and their wives. Each person takes a length of sugar cane and sits down in front of the seclusion house. The cane is pounded with a stick until the fibers in it are loose, then twisted and sucked until the juice runs copiously as the command "Milk come quickly, milk come plentifully" is uttered. This is the same method of extracting juice from sugar cane used by old people whose teeth are no longer strong enough to chew it, but for this ritual everyone mashes the cane with a stick regardless of how he eats it on other occasions because of the magical efficacy adhering in the abundant flow of juice that can only be produced by this method.

When the food has been cooked and a name has been decided on, the name is sent in to the mother along with a large platter of food. If the child is a girl, a miniature digging stick or net bag is placed atop the food, and if it is a boy a miniature bow or some arrows are included. These symbolize the major activities the child will engage in as an adult and are placed near the child to give it skill in these endeavors.

After the name of the child has been fixed, another ritual is performed. Part of it releases the father from various taboos and restrictions he has been subject to during the months of his wife's pregnancy and does not concern us here. The other part relates to the well-being of the new born child and involves the sibling, if any, who precedes it in birth order. The older child is made to sit down next to his father while an elderly male holds out to them large pieces of belly fat from the pig that has been killed. This portion of the pig is considered to be a great delicacy eating which solemnizes many occasions. The older child is expected to take several bites of this delicacy, and then he is rubbed with liquified pig grease and perhaps given a new ornament to wear. The Gururumba are well aware of the frustrations that can arise from sibling rivalry. They point out that an older sibling may have "bad thoughts" concerning the newly arrived addition to the family, and that these may enter the body of the newborn child to cause it illness or even death. The extra attention and place of prominence given the older sibling are aimed at forestalling the "bad thoughts" and thus protecting the infant. There is particular concern in the case where the siblings are males.

The various parts of this little series of rites can be understood as making symbolic statements about the lineage as a social unit and the place of the newborn infant in it. First, the protection given the young by the old is expressed through the concern they exhibit for the physical well-being of the child. This same concern is also expressive of the notion that the lineage as a whole, and not just the parents, are responsible for the growth and physical development of the child. Indeed, an important element in many life-crisis rituals performed by the lineage is an attempt to contribute to the growth of the individual by magical means. Second, the continuity of the lineage over time is expressed in the naming ceremony, for someone in the lineage gives the child his own name. People with the same name in a lineage call each other by a special term meaning "namesake," and a person who has given his name to a child will address the child's parents as "father of my namesake" or "mother of my namesake" rather than by their names or the appropriate kin term. A lineage, especially a large one, has a characteristic stock of names used over and over from one generation to the next. Finally, the potential threat to the unity of the lineage that the individual poses through the possibility of quarrels with a sibling is recognized, and the value of lineage unity is upheld in the face of this threat by a rite designed to reduce the possibility of such antagonism.

All the life-crisis rites manifest the same concerns, and it is significant that the performance of these rites is concentrated in the lineage, the only unit in Gururumba society having continuity over time that reproduces itself primarily from within rather than by recruitment or illiances with outside groups. The emphasis in lineage rites on the protection and growth of its human material thus becomes understandable.

The Ward and the Men's Cult

In previous chapters we have seen that the ward is partly a lineage group assuming common ancestry and partly a group of men arranged around a power figure. The ward is also the localized segment of a male secret cult organized around the ritual manipulation of sacred flutes.

Once every few years, all the boys in the ward between the ages of ten and fifteen are brought into the men's house to live. This is the beginning of an initiation ritual lasting for several months. There are many facets to this initiation, but only those relating to the flutes and induction into the male cult will be discussed here. When the boys enter the house they are neophytes. They are subject to a certain amount of teasing and must serve the older men in the house in various small ways. For example, the older men may announce that they are going to repay the boys for all the help they have given their elders in the past by working in the gardens, carrying wood and water, and the like. This is facetious because young boys are notable for their intractability when asked to assist in minor chores. Nonetheless, the men go off in a group to gather sugar cane which they bring back in bundles weighing several pounds each. When the boys are called out to receive their "compensation" and extend their arms for the cane, one bundle after another is piled on them until they collapse under the weight amid adult laughter. The boys are teased in many ways, all directed at their lack of cooperation in the past, their physical weakness, and their lack of sexual prowess. They are also lectured at various points about adult male responsibilities and are told they must begin preparing themselves physically to accept these responsibilities.

After spending a few days in the men's house the boys are brought together one night and the men remind them of times in the past when they have heard a strange sound said to be the call of a mystic bird. It is revealed to them that this sound was really made by pairs of men playing side-blown bamboo flutes. They are told they must learn to play these flutes, for doing so will make them physically, sexually, and behaviorally strong. The flutes are called *namo*, the generic term for "bird," and the boys are cautioned never to allow a woman to look upon the flutes. If a woman saw them it is said she would have to be killed. In the weeks to follow the boys will spend a great deal of time in a special enclosure deep in the forest learning to play these instruments.

The tunes the boys learn are limited in number, for each ward has a group of tunes belonging to it alone. If an adult hears flutes being played he can usually identify the ward affiliation of the players because of the distinctiveness of the tunes. The tunes have no particular story behind them, and their names refer to characteristics of the tonal or rhythmic pattern rather than to subject matter. The throbbing rhythm of a tune is most important, for it is thought to stimulate a substance in the body I will call vital essence and, thereby, growth, fertility, and strength. In addition to the initiation, the flutes are also played during various phases of two other rituals to be discussed below, called the *idzi namo* and *jaBirisi*. They are also manipulated in other ways as when they are fed, greased, decorated, hidden in garden houses, or put in association with other ritual objects to achieve their effect.

After the secret of the flutes has been revealed to them, the boys undergo a series of purification rites and observe a number of taboos whose purpose is to make them grow and become strong. The general idea behind all of them is that women can exercise a contaminating influence on men making them weak and even causing them illness. The efficacy of these rites and taboos depends, therefore, on separating the individual from all things female so he may develop without hindrance. Even after a boy becomes a man he will observe some of these taboos and occasionally purify himself in order to maintain the strength and other capacities the Gururumba deem necessary to function as an adult. The fact that men live separately from women much of the time is a further application of this idea.

The rituals of the men's cult embody two important principles: females can have a contaminating influence on males, and males can exercise ritual control over growth. The ward is the center of ritual activity relating to these principles, and whatever political, economic, or genealogical ties bind the members of the ward together are supplemented by common participation in the male cult. It should be noted in this context that the boys initiated together form a group of age mates, and individuals will call each other by a special term designating this relationship in preference to using a kin term obtaining between them.

The Sib and the Pig Festival

The pig festival is called *idzi namo* or "pig flute," and is a large-scale gift exchange occurring on the sib level at intervals of five or more years. In the festival a sib acts as host to one or more sibs belonging to neighboring tribes plus guests from distantly removed tribes. The main item in the exchange is pork, and the ceremony involves killing and cooking hundreds of pigs. The exchange is economically complex because it is structured in terms of both group and individual commitments. It is also politically complex because the fulfillment of these commitments in a grandiose, spectacular manner is an avenue to renown, and renown is one of the principles governing political action. Renown devolves on the organizers of the festival through its assertive display of strength in the piling up of vast amounts of food, vigorous discharge of obligations, and impressive pageantry. Finally, in addition to culminating a growth cycle by the killing of almost the total pig population and the depletion of gardens, it also starts a new growth cycle. Its ritual aspects can be seen as referring to both. In order to illustrate this, the use of flutes and gerua boards in the pig festival will be examined.

The *namo* flutes are blown and paraded during the preparations for the pig festival in ways that announce the achievement and strength of their owners. Their music signifies that the elusive processes involved in achieving growth, as evidenced in accumulated food and wealth, have been mastered. They are first sounded after the decision has been made to hold the festival, a second time when formal invitations are presented to guest groups, and a third time in the village of each man who accepts an invitation.

The flutes are also manipulated in certain ways to ensure that the vital power they control will continue to operate and produce another cycle of growth.

Thus, the flutes are wrapped in a leaf representing pigs so that when the flutes are played, real pigs will be stimulated to copulate and thus reproduce themselves. From time to time the flutes are also "fed" by placing bits of food in them in order that their power will not diminish. Finally, the flutes are placed in association with a wooden pole erected in a house on the ceremonial ground containing dance paraphernalia and other festival objects. This pole take on the power inherent in the flutes and the power acquired by the other objects through association with the pig festival. After the festival is over the pole is buried at some propitious spot in the sib territory so that its stored potency can regenerate the strength of sib members dissipated in the festival.

Another phase of the pig festival involves the display of *iNgErEBe*, or gerua boards, as they are usually called in the literature. These are wooden planks varying in size from a few inches to several feet in height painted with polychrome geometrical designs. One class is anthropomorphic in shape, but they usually are rectangular, square, round, or crescent-shaped. They are made ostensibly to honor the ghosts of the long dead, or ancestors, but their designs symbolize growth and the products of human endeavor.

The boards are worn or carried around the dance ground prior to the killing of the pigs. Amid the hundreds of people gathered for the occasion, the large numbers of pigs, the great piles of food, the boards move about on the shining bodies of children and youths laden with wealth in the form of feathers and shells. This juxtaposition of the boards and the accumulated wealth of the group is a tacit recognition of the dependence between the ancestors and their progeny. "The ancestors see the *iNgErEBe* and they know we have not forgotten them. They look and their bellies are good." There are special gerua dances done in imitation of the ancestors feverishly going about the work of raising pigs and gardens. Young children wearing gerua are allowed to "kill" a pig symbolically for the ancestors by striking it on the head with a red flowered bush which is a vegetable substitute for gerua board itself. Honoring the ancestors in this way ensures their continued contribution to the growth and vitality of the sib.

The designs on the boards symbolize prosperity and well-being, growth and vitality—qualities manifest in the pig festival itself. The markings on the boards represent things associated with wealth, display activities, and food. One design, called *girifoi*, represents the long strands of grass used to make brilliant bustles worn at dances where large amounts of food are given away. *Mondo numbuno* depicts the wooden cask for steaming food, food that nourishes both one's family and one's pigs. Another is *idzi oku'ne*, "pig skin," representing the marks made on a cooked, dressed pig before it is cut up into parts for distribution.

When the display is over, the boards are placed among the branches or trees in the gerua enclosure, a fenced area near the dance ground used in the pig festival. At times of crisis the boards may be removed and cleaned to stave off the harmful decaying forces manifest in sickness, death, and misfortune that periodically attack the sib.

The sib is the largest unit in Gururumba society acting as a unit in exchange affairs. The use of flutes and gerua boards in the pig festival is clearly aimed at maintaining the ability of the sib to engage successfully in exchange and, one might add, at maintaining a position of prominence in the wider scheme of intergroup relations.

The Phratry and the *jaBirisi* Ceremony

JaBirisi is a ritual centering around the ancestors performed by the phratry just prior to the pig festival or at times when it is judged that the phratry as a whole is experiencing difficulties. These difficulties include epidemics in the pig population; widespread illness among the people; difficulties with garden crops; and the general feeling that children are not growing rapidly enough. A factor in judging the seriousness of a crisis is the condition of the wooden structure around which the ceremony takes place. It is a circular fence fifteen to twenty feet in diameter and made of long, irregularly shaped posts. If this structure is dilapidated it is taken as a sign that the rite, which includes rebuilding and cleaning the structure, should be performed.

The rite begins with men going into the forest for several days to hunt for various small animals and birds. While the men are gone from the villages, taboos are placed on those remaining behind against doing "things the ancestors did not do." It is believed that in the time of the ancestors, man lived in a much simpler technological and social state than he does now so that there are taboos against making new fire or working in the gardens because the ancestors did not know how to do these things. When the men return from the forest, the animals they have collected are allowed to decompose partially and then are eaten in a village feast where the unsavory food is gobbled up in what the Gururumba consider to be a crude and disgusting fashion.

After this the taboos are lifted and the older men from various villages of the phratry gather at the *jaBirisi* structure to repair and clean it. When this is finished, pigs, which have been washed and decorated, are brought from all the villages of the phratry and killed at the structure, then cooked in earth ovens dug around its perimeter. All the food is then exchanged, each village giving some food to every other village. None of the food is sent outside the phratry as is usually done when large amounts of food are involved. As water is poured into the earth ovens, speeches are made calling on the ancestors to make things grow and flourish as they did in times past.

Both the structure and the rite are called *jaBirisi*, a term referring to plants characteristic of the forest as opposed to plants of the low-lands. Leaves of such plants are symbols of growth and fecundity and are used to induce these qualities in several kinds of rituals. Some of the *jaBirisi* structures are said to have stones buried in them. These stones, called ancestors, are thought to have been brought to their present location from the homeland of the phratry further down in the Asaro valley. The stones have a dual symbolism for they not only connect the present with the past, but they are in themselves symbols of permanence and indestructibility: they are used in the lightning exorcism ritual with expressly this meaning.

In addition to directly involving the ancestors and using symbols of growth and permanence, the rite also uses ritual drama to gain efficacy. This is done in two ways: First, the whole series of events is an enactment of the effect hoped for. It begins with the members of separate villages eating the rotting flesh of animals laboriously collected in the forest and ends with the consumption of well-larded pork freely exchanged among the members of a tribe. Connecting the ends of the rite is a renewal ceremony in which the decomposing fence housing the symbols of indestructibility is refurbished. Second, there is an attempt to achieve the aims of the ritual by symbolically participating in the course of human development, which the Gururumba see in terms of general improvement. Thus, the rite begins by imposing taboos that in effect return the community to its original unsophisticated state. The ritual as drama depicts the human group without the means of making fire, depending for subsistence on hunting small animals, and in general acting like primal men by gobbling half-rotten food. It ends with a bountiful spread of food, properly raised and cooked according to current methods. As one informant put it, "The men of long ago had nothing. They were like dogs. If we do as they did, we will increase as they did."

The phratry derives much of its identity from a sense of continuity with the past. This is not the recently known and experienced past, but the distant past of myth and the ancestors. When illness or misfortune strike the phratry and threaten its future, its link with the past, in the form of the ancestors, becomes a source of strength.

Groups and Rituals

Arranging a series of rituals according to the social level on which they occur is a device the ethnologist employs in understanding and explaining the rituals he observes in their relationship to social structure. The fact that each level of social grouping in Gururumba society has a ritual, or class of rituals, distinctive to it suggests to him the possibility of such an understanding. Furthermore, the symbolism of the rituals, and the aims they profess, manifest an "appropriateness" to the social level on which they occur. It is therefore understandable that the family has no ritual relations with the ancestors because the ancestors are seen as remote, distant figures and the family has no great genealogical depth. Beyond this, the juxtaposition of ritual forms and social forms allows the ethnologist to examine various ways the rituals may serve to stress values and ideals common to the group, or the way they bring the members of the group together in an activity of single, common purpose stressing their unity against factors that tend to divide them.

7

A Theme in Supernaturalism

"The Woman Showed Him the Flutes."

IN THE PRECEDING Chapter a set of rituals was arranged in such a way as to reveal relationships with social structure. In this chapter a set of rituals, beliefs, and taboos will be arranged so as to reveal their thematic interrelationships. Here I attempt to come closer to the meaning they have for the Gururumba.

The Concern with Growth and Strength

Just as it did not take long to formulate an impression that the Gururumba were "thing-oriented," so an impression of their great concern with growth and strength was formulated early in the field study. The Gururumba are horticulturalists and the growing of food is much on their minds. Casual conversation frequently turns around the state of one's garden or the health of one's pigs. Many of the songs they sing concern growth. These songs consist of very short stanzas, often simply one line, sung over and over in a variety of rhythmic and tonal patterns. Thus, the words of one song are, "The taro, its leaf unfolds." Another is, "Mothers, cut sweet potato vines, cut them!", and a third consists of "The bamboo shoot is growing." Similarly, some of the more elaborate string figures[1] depict plants or animals passing through phases in their growth cycle. A concern with physical strength is also manifest in everyday life, since a strong body is necessary for carrying out the tasks associated with gardening, hunting, and defending the group. It is a characteristic highly admired in both men and women, amounting to one of the major standards of beauty.

Concern with growth and strength is also evident in a number of small-scale rituals. For example, both men and women will rub themselves liberally

[1] These figures are made by manipulating string with the fingers to form patterns or designs recognizable as objects or animals. This "game" is very widely distributed throughout the world.

with stinging nettles or eat fresh ginger to stimulate strength before undertaking a difficult task. Men induce vomiting in themselves and bleed their noses for the same reason (these acts will be discussed more fully below). A man will spit into his son's mouth to make him grow rapidly, and a mother will put garlands of sweet potato vines around her daughter's head for the same purpose. Several kinds of rituals performed in connection with gardening manifest this concern, and a few examples will be presented to indicate their form.

First there are spells, in the form of commands, said over plants or over tools used in planting. They are quite simple, differing little from one another, but their secrets are jealously guarded. Some of these spells are "I am planting, I am planting!", "Grow taro, grow!", "You are the real climbing bean!", and "Sprout, sprout, out, out!." A few spells collected were said over the digging stick while it is being made. Except in one case where the spell was to prevent the maker of the digging stick from cutting himself while whittling the point of the tool—an event bringing misfortune to the garden—all were aimed at making the digging stick work quickly and efficiently.

Second, certain kinds of leaves and wood are placed in the ground to protect growing plants from insect pests or plant diseases and make plants mature rapidly. For example, a favorite method is to place a piece of dried betel nut shell in the earth piled up around each hillock of sweet potatoes. The Gururumba do not themselves chew betel as a rule, but their neighbors, the KErEmu, do, and it is from them that the nut husks are obtained. The Gururumba are aware of the slightly stimulating effect produced by chewing betel, and it is this quality that is drawn upon in planting the betel nut shells with sweet potatoes. Or, there is a kind of hardwood having a faintly unpleasant odor when freshly cut, large chunks of which are buried in the earth around the edges of a garden to keep the garden clear of insect pests: it is thought that the odor of the wood will keep them away. One might also include here the magic bundles tied to fence posts surrounding a garden for protection against thieves and marauding pigs. One such bundle consists of sweet-smelling grass twisted together into a short rope. Commands are "blown" into the grass where they are "held" by the odor. The commands, to bite and paralyze anyone coming over the fence who has no business in the garden, are thought to act of their own volition.

Finally are rituals performed after a garden has been planted to ensure its longevity. Stones are used for this purpose, drawing on their qualities of indestructibility and permanence as in the *jaBirisi* ritual. One method is to broadcast small stones around the garden while another is to bury a large stone near the center of the garden. In either case the object is to seed the garden with the quality of indestructibility and permanence.

The most complex ritual to promote the growth of plants is that for pandanus nuts. All the rites alluded to thus far can be performed by a single person, but the pandanus nut fertility ritual is performed by groups varying in size from the family to the sib. Furthermore, it does not have a series of variants which can be owned by individuals. Pandanus nuts are highly prized by the Gururumba, and during the nut-bearing season they largely abandon the normal routine of life in their lowland villages to move into the midmountain forest where the pandanus groves are located. These nuts are the Gururumba's only food resource that can be stored for long periods of time after harvesting. Some nuts are kept for three or four years after drying, and these are the most highly prized of all. The Gururumba do not fully understand the pattern of nut-bearing peculiar to the pandanus. They observe that in a particular grove in a particular season, some trees bear a nut head and others do not. Circumstances may be such that almost all the trees in a grove bear nuts or almost none bear them. They have noted this also. In an attempt to control this erratic growth pattern, they perform *mohin-gururu* in order to ensure that the trees that did not bear nuts in the current season will bear them in the next.

Part of the pandanus ritual consists of preparing food in an earth oven in honor of the ghosts of the recently dead. While the water is being poured in, speeches are delivered to the ghosts entreating them to "get inside" the barren trees and make them grow next season. The rest of the rite consists in building a kind of box on the ground near a pandanus grove and filling it with nut husks plus several kinds of leaves in an effort to stimulate the next season's growth. Two of these leaves are hot and peppery to the taste. They are "vitalizers" acting on the trees in much the same way that rubbing stinging nettles act on a person. Another of the leaves is thought to be particularly effective in attracting and holding the ghosts of the recently dead, while a fourth has a pungent odor capable of "capturing" commands spoken into it. The commands, which direct the trees to grow, are thus kept near the grove and work of their own efficacy on the trees. Other kinds of leaves added to the pile come from plants characteristic of the high forest. The forest is regarded as a fertile place; these leaves, imbued with its quality, become symbols of fertility. Moreover, in the context of the ritual they are thought to induce fertility.

Many other rituals aimed at inducing growth and strength can be recalled here from previous chapters. The playing of the flutes makes boys grow into men and causes pigs to reproduce. Gerua boards are cleaned in order to counteract forces that impede growth. The wooden pole put in contact with the paraphernalia of the pig festival stimulates strength in the sib. One aim of the *jaBirisi* is to restart the growth cycle brought to an end by the pig festival.

· Growth and Strength: Productivity and Assertiveness

A concern with growth and strength is manifested directly and simply in rituals like those involved in garden magic, but familiarity with larger, more complex rituals, such as the pig festival or male initiation, reveals growth and strength to be imbedded in a broader, more inclusive context. Thus, while it is true that the Gururumba are, in many instances, simply concerned that their gardens, pigs, and children should grow as a matter of survival, it is also true that achieving growth and showing strength have come to be values in their own right. The ability of an individual or group to be productive and asser-tive are among the most general values in Gururumba culture, and to produce food, to grow children, and pigs, to protect the group, to seek out and discharge obligations vigorously, is to demonstrate the presence of that ability. The rituals of growth and strength, then, are not only of importance to the Gururumba be-cause they add to their technical mastery of the physical world, but because they relate to the mastery of affairs in the social world as well.

This statement about the meaning of rituals dealing with growth and strength is an ethnological construction. The Gururumba do not speak so di-rectly and analytically about their own culture, but they do provide the clues recommending its plausibility. Some of these clues come from the simple straightforward acts of garden magic itself. Growing gardens in the upper Asaro valley is not particularly hazardous. In general there is a great deal of cer-tainty that when a crop is planted most of it will survive and flourish. How-ever, certain factors introduce an element of uncertainty into the situation. When the crops of one garden plot are becoming depleted while the crops of another are not yet mature, people may be short of food or have little variety in their diet. A pig may break into a garden and do a surprising amount of dam-age in a short time. There is a slight but persistent problem with insect pests, plant diseases, and theft. Thus, although the Gururumba do not live in an en-vironment hostile to their horticultural practices, these are areas where magic plays its role alongside technology. One other problem connected with garden-ing is dealt with by magic. People take pride in having a neat, abundantly pro-ductive garden. Moreover, to have such a garden is a sign that a man has the capacities for coping with life as the Gururumba understand it, and a man can gain or lose prestige according to the condition of his gardens. If a man's gar-den is near a main trail so that passers-by can easily see its quality, he may take ritual precautions to ensure its quality for this reason alone.

Other clues are to be found in the pig festival. Recall the meaning that the sounding of the flutes has in terms of announcing the strength and vitality of the sib. In speaking of this, one informant said, "The pig festival is no small matter, it is something of importance. The first time we sound the flutes, everyone hears us. When they hear it, they really know what we are like. They know we have watched after our pigs, our gardens, and have been active in trad-ing. They know we are strong and wonder at us." The very form of the pig fes-tival is calculated to have the same effect. The pigs to be given away are dis-played in long rows after they have been cooked, and the length of these rows will be remembered for years by the guests who use it as an index of group's strength. The other food and wealth objects are piled in massive displays for all to see, not simply brought forward at the moment of distribution. Sometimes an attempt is made to hold male initiation throughout the sib at the same time as the pig festival so that the newly initiated youths can be paraded before the guests as a show of the future strength of the group. Songs are sung by groups of dancing men, amounting to a public demonstration of the vital quality necessary for growing crops and pigs. The songs deal with growing food plants and exchange, and the dance consists of a mass of men who run in place for two or three hours without stopping. The pig festival is more than an exchange: it is a display of the fundamentally important capacity to be productive and assertive.

Productivity, Assertiveness, and Sexual Energy

Productivity and assertiveness are not simply personality traits for the Gururumba; they are behavioral characteristics stemming from a vital essence in the body which they call *gwondefoʃe*. In the broadest sense, this vital essence is the animating principle of the body, for death is the result of permanently losing it. Similarly, life is produced by combining substances that contain it. These two substances are semen and womb-blood, and they contain vital essence in slightly different forms: womb-blood in the form of amorphous life-principle, and semen in the form of vital material substance. Conception occurs when womb-blood is made solid and held in the body by semen, but menstruation occurs when it is not "solidified." In fact, menstrual blood becomes the antithesis of vital essence because it is regarded as dead womb-blood.

Vital essence is "hot," and as it courses through the body it causes affective states such as fear, anger, and sexual arousal. It also produces the physical strength of the body which allows men to grow food and protect the group, the behavioral assertiveness necessary for managing human affairs, and the capacity to reproduce the race.

In a very important sense, vital essence is identified with sexual energy. This can be seen by examining a list of bodily substances thought to contain it as opposed to those which do not. It is in semen and womb-blood, the two substances involved in conception, but is not in menstrual blood or in other genital secretions such as urine. It is in spittle and mother's milk. The viscous nature of the former is compared to semen by some informants, and the latter is a fluid only generated by the body in connection with childbearing. It is also in pubic hair and the beard hair of adult males, but not in other body hair. A full-grown beard is the sign of sexual maturity in males.

The connection between vital essence as the source of productivity and assertiveness and its identification with sexual energy is neatly exemplified by the fact that men are very much concerned about loss of semen and about being contaminated by menstrual blood. Semen loss occurs through excessive sexual activity or through having it stolen and transported to a sorcerer. Such a loss is of concern not only because it may eventuate in the loss of physical strength, manifested in general lassitude or illness, but also because it may impair one's ability to be assertive, as manifested by a decline in personal fortune. Thus, a man believes himself to be sorcerized not simply because he is ill—he believes it because his pigs are not growing, his wife has left him, and he finds he cannot meet exchange demands being made on him. The ultimate reason for all this is that he has lost semen, which means he has lost vital essence. Similarly, menstrual blood is contaminating because it is antithetical to vital essence, and women must be very careful to dispose of it lest a man, or a pig, come in contact with it. Such contact would produce illness, but the Gururumba do not see this as an attack on their bodies so much as on their capacity to function as human beings.

These connections can also be seen in the symbolism and ritual surrounding first menstruation. A relatively full account of this event will follow to demonstrate the connections. When a girl first menstruates she tells her mother, who calls the news out to the girl's father. It quickly becomes a matter of public knowledge, and it is important that it be so, for no male may enter the house where the girl must stay during the course of this first menstruation.

During the days the girl is secluded in the house, she is under certain restrictions. She must not go outside except at night, and then only briefly, because she is considered to be so dangerous that any male seeing her would become ill. Similarly, she must not touch herself or eat with her fingers because she can be dangerous even to herself. She is made to sit on a layer of leaves and moss so that the blood can be collected and carefully disposed of lest it come in contact with a male or a pig and cause illness. She must not drink water since it might "cool" the "hot" sexuality developing within her and rob her of procreative abilities.

During this time she is constantly attended and made aware of how carefully she must act in the future to guard the community against the contaminating influence of succeeding menstruations. She hears tales of misfortune befalling men and pigs because some woman did not properly dispose of her menstrual blood. She learns that she must never step over food because she may contaminate it, nor may she straddle a stream or hand food directly to anyone for the same reason. A day or two before it is expected she will emerge from seclusion to ensure the potency of her reproductive powers, her father prepares a ritual meal consisting of beetle grubs, roasted and sprayed with masticated *gimbi* (tree bark) and *gafu' gifiri* (a nut). Ingestion of the grubs and the tree bark ensures the growth of many children, and the nut, which has a peppery taste, is a vitalizer making her active after her confinement.

Soon after this the girl emerges from the house and a final rite is performed. As part of the preparation for this rite the path leading from the seclusion house to a nearby earth oven is thickly covered with leaves of several kinds: *afagule, akumaku, gwonumbu' gini,* and *morEnge.* The first three are species of *Cordyline* (tanket), and the last a variety of *Setaria palmiforlia* (edible pitpit). Tanket leaves are used in several ritual contexts as symbols of growth and productivity. This derives in part from their remarkable ability to take root from even apparently dry pieces of stalk, and in part from their association with gardens where they are used as boundary markers. *Afagule* with its red midrib and *akumaku* with its red edges are said to represent menstrual blood, but in this ritual they emphasize the positive rather than the negative side of menstruation.

Menstrual blood is itself dangerous, but menstruation is the sign that reproduction is possible, that the vital energy that produces children and gardens exists. *Gwonombu' gini* are such a deep shade of green as to appear black, and thus representing pigs whose skins are black. *MorEnge* has a firm but pliable stalk and is used to prepare a girl's vagina for sexual intercourse by repeated manipulations that enlarge the vaginal opening and break the hymen.

When the leafy path has been completed, and other things are in readiness, the girl is brought out of the house. Two men, each carrying one end of a long piece of sugar cane approach the door of the house. They split the cane for most of its length leaving only the ends intact. The ends are then pushed together so that the two halves of the cane bulge apart forming a hoop. The split cane is held in front of the door, and a third man crawls into the house. Taking the girl by the hand he leads her out and through the hoop making sure her body comes in contact with the juicy cane. This act is compared to the emergence of a butterfly from its cocoon, and it is also said that the sweet juices of the cane will attract suitors from a great distance. The girl stands on the leaf-strewn path holding the hands of her guardian and of her father's brother while listening to a speech concerning marriage; then she is led down the path to become the center of attraction at a food exchange.

These rites at once celebrate the onset of reproductive powers in a girl, magically assist in its development, and symbolize the several modes of its expression in everyday life. The celebrative aspect is evident in the seclusion period as well as in the terminal feast. During seclusion the girl becomes the object of much attention as old women, age mates, and prepubescent girls gather to give advice, instruction, or just to stare. The focus of their conversation is on the new potency within her and how it is to be handled. The terminal feast is in part a public announcement that a girl has reached sexual maturity and is now capable of assuming adult status through marriage, and in part a celebration of achievement by the community that grew her. The new power she has is not simply left to its own course of development and expression, however: It has to be made prolific by feeding the girl the bark of a coniferous tree notable for its abundant display of seed cones; it has to be turned to developmental growth by feeding her grubs notable for their ability to change from amorphous pupae to intricate insects; its negative expression in menstruation has to be limited by imposing taboos. Finally, the symbolism stresses the dual meaning of this power in the narrow sense of sexuality and the wider sense of productivity. The seclusion period is a time for the open discussion of intercourse outside the circle of a girl's age mates. Older women encourage her to prepare her vagina for it and men spread *morEnge* on the path she trods after seclusion. There are, in addition to the sugar cane hoop, several other magical devices to make the girl attractive to males. But the path she trods also contains leaves symbolizing growth, gardening, and pigs. These are the productive concerns to which she must turn her vital energies in adult life. She observes similar restrictions in subsequent menstrual periods so that the health and well-being of the community can be preserved.

Male and Female Sexuality

The rather puzzling notion that women can contaminate men has been mentioned several times in the preceding sections, and it may have occurred to the reader that this indicates a kind of institutionalized antagonism between the sexes. It would be a mistake to see the symbolism of the rituals we have been discussing in this light, however. Male–female represent complementary not antagonistic forces for the Gururumba, and the rituals deal with differing kinds of control over them rather than with their opposition. This can be seen by describing more fully the rituals of male initiation and comparing them with those just described concerning first menstruation.

After the secret of the flutes has been revealed to the boys, a second phase of male initiation occurs. In it the boys are introduced to further ritual techniques contributing to their growth and vitality by ridding their bodies of contaminating substances. Men have two such contaminating substances in their bodies: menstrual blood, which males inadvertently ingest while in their mother's womb, and the remnants of food given them by women in the period prior to moving into the men's house. This blood, which is contaminating because it is dead, is purged by bleeding the nose. This is accomplished by pushing small bundles of sharp-edged grass in and out the nostrils. The resultant bloody flow is said to be equivalent to menstruation, and informants explicitly refer to the act as "our (male) menstruation." Food, contaminating because it may have been touched by a menstruating woman, is purged by vomiting. This is induced by placing a piece of bent cane in the mouth, forcing it down the throat into the stomach, then working it up and down until vomiting occurs. The first time the cane is swallowed it is also said to break a tissue somewhere inside the body. The Gururumba consider that this tissue must be pierced before the penis will grow properly or semen will form. In later life males employ both these techniques to purify themselves after possible contamination or to strengthen themselves before undertaking difficult tasks.

There is a final phase of male initiation in which food taboos, behavioral restrictions, and a strict life regimen are imposed on the boys. Some of these last for about a year, some until marriage is consummated, and some until they are old men. During this final phase they cannot accept any food from the hand of a woman, any food grown by women, or any food distributed at ceremonies connected with pregnancy and birth. They should generally avoid contact with women; if one of the group of boys initiated together is betrothed during this period, they all must carefully avoid the bride-to-be as well as the betrothed boy. These restrictions last for about a year, except the one against accepting food at pregnancy or birth ceremonies, which lasts until the boy himself becomes a husband. They must also refrain from eating lizards, snakes, frogs, and salamanders for these creatures are said to feed on menstrual blood, a taboo that continues until old age. During the ensuing months the boys lead a Spartan life; each morning they purify themselves by vomiting in a nearby stream; they bathe in cold water; their noses are bled frequently and their bodies rubbed with stinging nettles; their diet is restricted to bananas, sugar cane, and greens from the forest (male food). Boys say of this time, "We eat nothing but the vomiting cane." All these things are done to make their bodies grow strong and vital. They also spend long hours practicing on the flutes in a specially built structure deep in the forest.

Male and female initiation are similar in that they both are importantly concerned with the sexual potency and growth of the body, but they differ in the way this concern is manifested. Female initiation celebrates the fact of growth and the onset of reproductive power and deals symbolically with the latter's nonsexual aspects. Control of this power is not a problem except as it may adversely effect others. In male initiation the principal aim is to induce growth and reproductive power, not celebrate its existence. Controls are for the good of the initiate rather than the good of others. The Gururumba point out that newly initiated boys are not equivalent to girls who have recently menstruated because the boys are not yet strong enough to cope with the vital sexuality of these girls. To have contact with them for sexuality, even in such an innocuous form as a pregnancy feast, would stop the boys' growth and impair the development of their own vital essence. Until they have developed a full growth of beard they must continue to strengthen themselves through ritual or protect themselves through avoidances; even after that they must continually guard against the contaminating and weakening influences of sexual activity. In initiation, then, males assume a ritual control over the same vital power that females assume a natural control over when they menstruate for the first time.

From all this material we can conclude that for the Gururumba there is a kind of fundamental disparity between the sexes because women are naturally endowed with reproductive capacity, which is the working of the vital essence in them. This disparity is overcome in the rituals of the male secret cult aimed at generating and maintaining the productive capacity, which is the working of the vital essence in man. In effect, men reproduce symbolically all the important elements given naturally to women: the flutes are reproductive power, nose bleeding is menstruation, and breaking the tissue during the first vomiting is breaking the hymen. It is interesting in this connection that the myth told in explanation of the origin of the flutes specifies that it was a woman who revealed their secrets to men.

This myth tells of a young boy forced by an old woman to accompany the men into the forest to collect animals for a *jaBirisi*. The boy, who is really too small for such a task, gathers up a ragged net bag, a small bow, a few reed arrows, and sets out for the forest. Deep in the woods he meets a woman. She recognizes his pitiable situation, throws away his inefficient implements, and invites him to come to her house. There she lives alone surrounded by a magnificent garden including all the plants traditionally grown by men. After giving him gifts, she shows him how to make traps and place them along animal trails. That night, while the boy sleeps, the woman fills the traps with animals she has caught herself, and repeats this on the second night. In succeeding days the two prepare other foods to be used in the *jaBirisi* including pigs which the woman pulls up out of the ground. On the day before returning to the village, she teaches him to play the flutes, and when they play together he is transformed into a young man. On their way to the village the woman tells the young man to make her a knife for peeling sweet potatoes, but cautions him to make it of dried rather than green bamboo. The young man forgets this interdiction, and the woman cuts her finger while using the knife. When the blood flows she disappears. The young man follows the bloody trail back into the forest because he plans to marry the woman, but finds she has turned into a tree kangaroo and will not change back because he disobeyed her command. He thus loses a wife but gains the flutes.

This myth is not only interesting because it identifies a woman as the original source of the flutes, which supports the notion that male rituals are the equivalent of natural female endowments, but also because of the kind of being she is. She is a total human: her knowledge of trapping, her tending of male plants, and her possession of the flutes are all male attributes, and yet she is female. It is also noteworthy that she is not an ogre or dangerous being, but is generally nurturant. These features can be taken as a symbolic statement concerning the fundamental complementarity of the sexes in achieving life-sustaining goals.

One more fact can be introduced at this point illustrating the complementarity of the sexes and the identification of vital essence with sexual energy. All the rituals and taboos relating to male control over female reproductive power and the possibility of female contamination do not obtain throughout life but only during the reproductive years. This is the only period when the natural potency of females may hold some danger for males. Thus we find that old men can once more eat frogs, lizards and snakes, and we also find that old women are sometimes made guardians of the flutes. It is careful control over reproductive power, the well-spring of human energy, that is emphasized in these rituals and beliefs rather than male-female antagonism.

Body and Cosmos

If an ethnologist observing contemporary Americans attempted to characterize the way they dealt with their physical environment, he would probably stress the point that the man-nature relationship is mediated primarily by technological means. The resources used to wrest from the environment the things deemed necessary are tools, technological knowledge, and nonhuman energy sources. For the Gururumba, on the other hand, the man–nature relationship is probably best characterized as mediated by man's own body. They make tools and possess a corpus of technological knowledge, but there is no nonhuman energy source known to them. Ultimate control over nature therefore rests on control over the energy source in their own bodies, and this, we have argued, is primarily sexual in nature.

Additional support for this characterization comes from an examination of Gururumba notions concerning nature. The immediate physical environment is an object of interest for the Gururumba. The flora and fauna are well known to them, and they name, classify, and have a body of knowledge about life forms which is quite impressive. Their interest is largely oriented to utilitarian ends and plant classification is in terms of use rather than morphology. This utilitarian orientation to nature is not the sole interest they display in it intellectually, however, as indicated by the existence of such things as a large body of knowledge concerning the life cycle and habits of insects which has little uilitarian application.

The more remote objects of nature are of little interest to the Gururumba. The sun, although referred to in a few myths and sometimes depicted on gerua boards or war shields, is not an important figure in their system of supernatural entities. In myths, the sun is always a secondary character, if personified at all, and none of the myths are specifically about the sun. The Gururumba know the sun gives warmth and contributes to plant growth, but they do not see it as an all-powerful force in nature, nor do they even care to speculate about its apparent movements. Much the same is true of the moon, stars, meteorites, the wind, rain, and other aspects of the cosmos. There is no world creator in Gururumba myth.

What we think of as nature simply consists of the immediate physical environment for the Gururumba. It is not a vast machine understood mechanically, nor is it an apparent reality understood in terms of hidden, mystic forces. It is a "thing" which man manipulates and contends with, using the vital forces within himself. As the corpus of ritual discussed in this chapter reveals, controlling man's body means controlling the rest of nature. The only myth hero the Gururumba have is a male being who passed through the Asaro valley teaching men how to grow yams and taro, and whose body sprouted plants when he died. The important aspects of the cosmos are inside man's body, not outside it.

8

A View of Man and Society

"We are like pigs."

IN ADDITION TO the rituals concerned with control of man's vital energies, the Gururumba also have a series of beliefs postulating the existence of entities and forces we would call supernatural. Some of these, nature spirits and ancestors, have already been mentioned, but there are others as well, and their characteristics will be presented below. The entities do not form any very obvious system, as in a hierarchy of gods for example, but they can be viewed as systematically related to the notion of vital essence. Furthermore, in combination with other material they can be used as clues to assumptions the Gururumba make about their own human nature.

It should be mentioned at this point that our use of the notion "supernatural" does not correspond to any Gururumba concept: they do not divide the world into natural and supernatural parts. Certain entities, forces, and processes must be controlled partially through *lusu,* a term denoting rituals relating to growth, curing, or the stimulation of strength, while others need only rarely be controlled in this way. Entities falling within this realm of control are here included in our "supernatural." However, *lusu* does not contrast with any term denoting a realm of control where the nature of the controls differ from *lusu.* Consequently *lusu* is simply part of all control techniques, and what it controls is simply part of all things requiring human control.

The Realm of *Lusu*

Rituals and taboos relating to the control, stimulation, or protection of vital essence are referred to as *lusu.* The notion of vital essence has already been discussed a length, and only a few aspects need be added here. Humans are not the only creatures animated by vital essence, for pigs and dogs are thought to have it as well. In fact, there is a ritual designed to capture the departing vital essence of a dying pig in order to introduce it into a living pig to make it grow

83

faster and larger. It consists of passing a sweet potato around the dead pig's body; the essence enters the potato which is then fed to another pig. Death may result from a variety of sorcery techniques acting on vital essence. The sorcery performed on semen has already been mentioned, but there are other techniques such as one that pulls vital essence out of the body. When a person is asleep his vital essence passes in and out of his relaxed body upon inhaling and exhaling. A clever sorcerer is able to hold a little noose in front of a sleeping person's nose, tighten it around his vital essence as it protrudes from the nose, and pull it out. Another technique "cools" the "hot" essence by magically shooting mud balls into a person's viscera. Cigarette smoke, which is "cool," is used with the same effect by blowing it on a person.

When a person dies his physical body ceases to function, but the vital essence that animated him continues to exist in the incorporeal form of a ghost (*foroso*). These ghosts remain in contact with the living members of the village and sib, but the general effect they have on the living is undesirable: serious lingering illnesses, accidents, trouble with pigs, the occurrence of rain storms at inappropriate times, madness, and death. The ghost of a person recently deceased has to be driven away from the community by shouting at it and exploding segments of green bamboo lest it remain in close and dangerous association with the living, but it does not go far and stays close by the place where its body is buried. The most frequent actions on the part of the living toward ghosts are ritual attempts to dissuade them from disruptive activity. Ghosts may also be helpful toward the living, but acts of this type are infrequent and have consequences of only minor importance. They appear in dreams, usually to predict death or misfortune, but occasionally to reveal new kinds of garden magic or new magic to cure illness in pigs. They may also halt impending rain and keep intruders out of gardens, but they cannot be depended on to do these things nor are they frequently enjoined to do them.

Examination of cases in which ghosts have caused illness, death, injury, or madness reveals some rationale in the seemingly capricious behavior of ghosts, although it may not be immediately apparent. Here, for example, is an instance of ghostly attack that seems to indicate that ghosts attack people for little or no reason at all, yet falls into a classifiable pattern as shown below.

A party of men from the village of Miruma had gone into the high mountain forest to search for wild pandanus nuts. While there, some of them decided to go hunting for tree-climbing kangaroos. They left the camp, but returned in a few hours without any kills, only BoNgire did not return. The men were beginning to wonder what had happened to him when suddenly he burst into camp. He was bleeding at the nose and his body was badly scratched. He rushed to the edge of the campfire where he stood for a moment without saying anything, then quite unexpectedly began shouting wildly and attacking anyone within reach. He was quite agitated and it took several men to restrain him. He was finally subdued and tied to a tree at the edge of the clearing. Judging from this behavior it was decided that he had been attacked by a ghost. At this point what had happened could not be ascertained for BoNgire continued to shout and speak incoherently and no one could communicate with him. Accordingly, the fire was built up a bit, and then smothered with wet leaves to create smoke. BoNgire was then suspended from a pole, in much the same way as when a pig is carried from one place to another, and was held in the smoke until he began to choke and vomit. Finally, after about five minutes of this treatment, he cried out in normal speech to be taken out of the smoke. This signalized that the dangerous contact with the ghost had been exorcised from him and that he was once more normal. A short time later, BoNgire was able to give his own account of what happened. He said, "I was in the forest looking for a tree-climbing kangaroo. I looked up into a tree and saw a nest. I knew there would be a tree kangaroo in it. I climbed the tree next to the tree with the nest. I went up. I kept on going up. When I got to the top I could see there was a tree kangaroo in the nest. I did not have my bow. I called to Usi [a man BoNgire had gone into the forest with and whom he thought was nearby] to come up the tree with his bow. I called Usi several times [Usi had gone back to camp]. I said his name, but he did not come. Then I saw Usi's namesake in the tree with me [the ghost of a departed village mate with the same name], and he was red. Usi's namesake said, "Why do you keep calling my name? I do not like to have my name called.' Then he bit me. I fell out of the tree. He kept on biting me. I could not see, I could not hear."

In other cases ghosts attack because they want to have their bones cleaned, because their graves are being disturbed by soil slippage or dampness, because no one mentioned their name at the last pig festival, because they are lonely, or simply because they feel like it.

One fact is quite clear from the material on ghostly attack: ghosts do not attack because they are punitive or vengeful. Informants were asked specifically if ghosts would attack a person who had committed some act considered wrong, and the answers were consistently in the negative. In other words, ghosts are not moral agents punishing the living for acts of wrongdoing. Neither are they thought of as vengeful. Wrong between living individuals is not made right by ghostly attack when the wronged individual dies and becomes a ghost. In general terms, ghosts act because of affonts to their physical person, as in the case of wanting their bones cleaned; to their esteem, as in the case of not wanting to be forgotten; or to express some strong personal desire, as in the case of not wanting to have one's name spoken. There is no taboo against speaking the names of the dead, and when BoNgire was attacked it was because the ghost of Usi simply did not want his name called out. The Gururumba regard ghostly attack as stemming primarily from their overbearing self-assertiveness: that's just the way ghosts are.

Foroso are the ghosts of the recently dead, the dead whose names are known. Ancestors (*aBwaho*) are the ghosts of the long dead, whose names are no longer known or were never known. Ancestors have been mentioned previously in connection with the *jaBirisi* ritual which is classed as *lusu*. To call these beings ancestors is slightly misleading since that term usually denotes the known dead to whom specific genealogical connections can be traced. *ABwaho*, on the other hand, are not known as individuals but only as a group. They are like "forefathers" or "founders of the race," and ritual contact is made with them only as a group. Unlike ghosts they are distant rather than near figures, they do not enter directly into the affairs of a person, nor are they "seen" as "ghosts frequently are.

The Gururumba think of the ancestors as having two quite distinct sets of characteristics. As we have seen they regard the ancestors as sources of the vital energy necessary to grow food and children. They speak of them with admiration for having produced the present generations of men and depict them in songs and dances as busily engaged in growing food and children. At the same time they place their existence in a distant past when human society and culture was not as it is now. Men did not have domesticated plants and animals and did not live within the bounds of a society but as social isolates. They raped, murdered, and stole as whim directed them and ranged freely over the countryside without concern for boundaries. On the one hand, then, their vital energies are manifested in generally nurturant concerns, on the other, in strong assertive behavior that amounts to aggression.

The term *lusu* also applies to rituals curing illness caused by witches and to divinatory techniques for finding witches. Witches are called *gwumu,* this term also being applied to a substance inside them causing them to be witches. The term comes from the root verb meaning to steal. Witches can fly through the air, change shape, and get inside things, including the body of a human or pig. They usually attack by eating the liver, which is the main seat of vital essence, but they also eat the flesh of fresh corpses. They "mark" their victims by pushing small sticks into the ground near the intended target and project themselves into the victim by changing into insects or reptiles with mystic powers. They also have superpowerful garden magic at their command.

The outstanding characteristic of witches is their inordinate acquisitiveness and envy of others. Witches get inside packets of food given at gift exchanges and gobble it up before the recipient can get the bundle home. Witches grow superabundant gardens simply as a means of shaming others rather than to provide food for the family or the exchange group. Witches attack the pigs of others because the pigs belong to others rather than to themselves. They attack elaborately decorated dancers, good warriors, or handsome persons out of envy. They steal food from gardens and valuables from houses because they want them. The eating of corpses falls into this pattern also because the Gururumba explain it as a desire to acquire meat beyond any normal human needs. *Gwumu* is such a voracious force it may even destroy the body it inhibits.

There are two other important characteristics of witches. First, they are real in the sense that actual persons are occasionally accused of being witches. Second, witches are generally thought to be females, all the serious accusations of witchcraft being made against women. If a real witch is found, she may be killed or may commit suicide before any action can be taken. On the other hand, she may admit guilt and be willing to pay compensation for damage done and thus escape serious harm; or the witch may be "rehabilitated" through a rite of exorcism which rids her body of the witch substance.

Accusations of witchcraft are frequently made in the heat of argument and such accusations are made of men as well as women. Serious accusations involving a concerted attempt to find the witch are only made against women, however. There is the belief that men may consort with witches but they do not thereby become witches. They can gain certain benefits from such contact as indicated in the following statement:

A witch can turn into many things; birds, dogs, another person. If a man sees a witch turning into something else he should go up to her afterwards and tell her he knows she is a witch. She will offer to give him some valuable thing such as a shell if he lets her alone and does not tell anyone else. He must refuse. Then she will say that he can fondle her breasts if he does not tell. He must refuse. Then she will say that he can have sexual intercourse with her if he does not tell. A wise man will refuse this also and ask for a piece of her hair or a piece of her string apron. He will take it and hide it in a tree or under a stone so that others cannot find it. In the time of warfare he could bring it out, wrap it around sugar cane and burn it. Rubbing the ashes in his hair would make enemy arrows miss him. Now it could be used in court cases. A head man can ask someone else to do this for him if a court case is coming up.

Lusu is also used to cure illness caused by harmful thoughts. It may happen that the bad thoughts one person harbors about another leave his head and enter the body of the other person where they cause illness or even death. An individual cannot will his thoughts to do this, nor can he restrain them from doing it; it just happens. Although the Gururumba do not comment on it, illness or death from this cause occurs exclusively between village mates or sib mates who have had a serious argument without its erupting into physical violence. Blame is not placed on the person whose bad thoughts did the harm, for it is felt that they were partially caused by the actions of the other person. The cure for illness caused in this way brings together the two people involved so that each may rub the other with water in which some valuable object has been immersed.

Nature spirits are also within the realm of *lusu*, but they do not need to be discussed further. The only remaining force of any consequence to the Gururumba that is dealt with by *lusu* is lightning. Lightning is not personified, but when it strikes a tree owned by someone it is thought to remain in the tree as a malignant force which can cause harm to the owner of the tree or some member of his immediate kin group. It is especially dangerous to "weak" men, men who are ill or who are not close to the male ideal of assertiveness and strength. Such a threat is met by a ritual exorcising the lightning and strengthening the persons potentially in danger. Like any kind of illness caused by agents discussed in this chapter, a lightning strike is of concern because of its effect on a person's vital energy, and thus his ability to be an effective person, which explains the emphasis on strengthening in this rite although no one is actually ill.

These, then, are the major supernatural forces and entities postulated by the Gururumba. Although they differ in form, abode, and other features, the similarities in the way they enter into human affairs are of interest here. First, they are viewed as involved directly rather than remotely in human affairs. They are not of importance to the Gururumba because they created the world or significant parts of it, nor because they are the forces that run the natural order, nor because they are the guardians of the moral order. Rather, they are of importance because they affect an individual's capacity to cope effectively with the demands and opportunities he meets in daily existence. The fact that ghosts cause illness is not meaningful to the Gururumba because it explains illness or because it is a punishment for moral transgression; it is meaningful because it robs a woman of the strength necessary to carry out her daily tasks in the garden or deprives a man of the vigor needed in social intercourse. Second, insofar as these entities and forces exercise a benevolent influence on human affairs it is through the contribution they make to productive activity. This may occur, as with spirits, in the form of directly participating in some task or, as with vital essence, in the form of the forceful energy needed to carry out any enterprise. Conversely, these entities and forces are regarded as malevolent when they impede productive activity. It is significant in this regard that illness or death is always regarded as only one element in a general pattern of personal misfortune when one of these entities is thought to be the cause.

The realm of *lusu* can be seen as that in which positive control is exercised over entities and forces affecting man's capacity to be productive and assertive: it protects and nourishes. Its opposite is not the realm of the natural but of sorcery in which negative control is exercised: it attacks and destroys. There is no single term for sorcery, only a series of terms for classes of sorcery techniques. None of them are classed as *lusu*, nor are rituals for counteracting sorcery called *lusu*. Some parts of such a ritual, those dealing with symptoms but not with cause, may be referred to in this way; the specialist who performs the ritual is called *lusuBe*. Sorcery is not practiced against persons in one's own village or sib, nor are its techniques mysterious as are those of witchcraft. Some sorcery is known by almost every adult, and it can be purchased or sold like any object. *Lusu* relates to gardening and exchange partners, sorcery to warfare and enemies.

System in the Realm of *Lusu*

We have spoken above about the importance of productivity and assertiveness to the Gururumba. Much of the character of Gururumba life can be understood as if it were the result of striving to attain these ends. More particularly, it can be understood as if it were an attempt to achieve some balance between nurturant and destructive tendencies in man—an attempt to turn strength into nurturant channels. To a Westerner, daily life among the Gururumba appears to be carried on in a highly aggressive fashion: the constant banter about giving and taking, the frequency of fights and violent emotional eruptions, and the fact that many of the idioms in the language are built around "violent" verbs such as "hit," "strike," or "kill." "I hit him" can mean "I gave it to him," rather than the reverse as in our own language. In most contexts this kind of behavior is not aggression to the Gururumba; it is a display of the strength stemming from vital essence, the strength man draws upon to endure and flourish. Within that part of the social world defined by the sharing of food, assertiveness is not aggressiveness because it creates food and the social channels through which food flows. Furthermore, making a demand implies the obligation to be demanded of, and giving is not a means of overwhelming others because reciprocity will transform givers into takers. The possibility of gift exchange becoming a competitive spiral is thus held in check by striving for a balance between nurturance and strength.

There are several ethnographic facts illustrating this tendency toward balance and reciprocity. Repayment of a debt should be equivalent to the amount lent, no more nor less. Games, and certain kinds of warfare, should end in a tie rather than victory. The difficulty of achieving this when both sides strive to display strength accounts for the fact that games, such as a rough and tumble version of soccer introduced by Australians, may go on for several days. Finally, there is the interesting elaboration of the notion of compensation. Compensation can be demanded for injuries received while working for another, the damaging of tools or objects lent to another, or for damage done to gardens by another's pigs or children. In addition, compensation may be demanded for dancing too well at someone else's food distribution or for giving a food distribution of a more elaborate nature than expected by the guest. Thus, within a certain social context failure to achieve the proper balance has its cost, for a person 'injured" in this way will appear before the men's house weeping and crying loudly that he has been "killed" by the offenders and he must then be taken into the house, fed, greased, and presented with valuables.

If one accepts this as an accurate characterization, then the supernatural entities and forces postulated by the Gururumba can be seen as conjoined in a system expressing balances and imbalances of strength and nurturance.

We can start with the notion of vital essence and view it as an expression of the most perfect balance between nurturance and strength. The hot substances flowing in the body make a person physically, sexually, and behaviorally strong. Within the food-exchanging community this display of strength is not destructive. The assertion of physical strength protects the group from enemy onslaught by force of arms and enables men and women to carry out the heavy tasks associated with providing food and shelter. A man acts assertively in the sexual act by having intercourse repeatedly, but this is in order to bind firmly the substance that will develop into the child he is helping to grow. When his sexual energies are not helping to develop his child, they must be conserved and protected so they can contribute strength to the performance of other productive tasks including the forceful fulfillment of obligations that leads to renown for the individual and group.

The notions of ghost and harmful thought express a harmful imbalance between strength and nurturance created when strength is focused primarily on self-assertion. Ghosts act in an overbearing, "pushy" manner to make their own desires and needs known. They are not linked with one another or with the living in striving for common goals, nor is their assertiveness connected in any significant way with productive activity. They are "strong" without being nurturant and are harmful in that they display strength unmodulated by the limiting factors of reciprocity and obligation. A ghost is vital essence released from the social forces that directed it into nurturant channels and consequently turned to forcing others to recognize it as a self. Assertiveness, even within the context of reciprocity and obligation, can also lead to harm as indicated in the notion of harmful thoughts. People can harm one another in the course of everyday events simply because of the assertiveness normally inherent in their actions. Strength and nurturance may be balanced in each man, but when men interact the forcefulness characterizing their behavior can bring about unintentionally harmful consequences.

The notion of nature spirit expresses a harmful imbalance between strength and nurturance created when strength is focused on concern with objects and rights of ownership, or when sexual energy becomes lust. Nature spirits seek out opportunities to copulate with human females, but their interest in females is fornicative, not procreative. Similarly, they watch over pigs, gardens, and territory because they are "theirs" rather than because they are needed resources. Nurturance, insofar as it means an interest in growth and feeding, is separate from strength in nature spirits, but they can be made to work for the good of man if their proprietary interests are taken into account. Spirits are helpful or harmful largely to the extent that their proprietary interests are either taken into account or ignored. Having such interests is not harmful in itself, but ignoring such interests in others may lead to harm.

The characteristics attributed to ancestors are interesting in terms of our interpretation because they suggest a fundamental separation of nurturance from strength in human nature that is only resolved through the agency of society. When ancestors are spoken of as giving free reign to their impulses and living by their individual wits and strength, they are described as living in a presocial era. Informants typically say of this period that it lacked institutions of marriage and gift exchange, and point out that the ancestors did not live in villages. When ancestors are spoken of as busily engaged in producing food and growing children, however, it is always within a social context since the food is grown by the combined labor of men and women, and because it is depicted as used in exchange activities. The behavior of the presocial era the Gururumba call strong; we might refer to it popularly as motivated by "the baser instincts." The notion of ancestors can be seen as an institutionalized recognition that man has such "base instincts." To anticipate the next section somewhat, this interpretation is especially borne out by the fact that informants spontaneously suggested in a variety of contexts that they would be like ancestors of the presocial era if they did not have to live in the company of other men.

The notion of witchcraft expresses a separation of strength from nurturance that cannot be resolved within the food-producing unit. The outcome is aggression. Witches are similar to ghosts in certain respects, but ghosts can be placated while witches cannot. When a ghost attacks it is to make its desires known or its presence felt, and its attacks cease when these desires have been fulfilled or its presence recognized. Ghostly attacks can be seen as the means whereby ghosts maintain their self-esteem and identity through the display of strength in the form of self-assertion. The Gururumba do not view witches as being concerned with their self-esteem or identity. A witch makes no demands and gains a general satisfaction through the attack itself rather than a specific satisfaction from the results of the attack. Witches not only manifest strength without nurturance, they turn strength into aggression since their actions have no purpose, not even assertion of the self. Lightning is witchcraft's counterpart in nature. It is destructive to no particular end, striking at points of weakness like the trees of a sick man, rather than points of strength like a handsomely decorated dancer.

A correspondence between this characterization of witches and general attitudes concerning the position of women within the sib partially explains why women, rather than men, are regarded as witches. Men point out that women do not really care about planning and preparing lineage- or sib-sponsored food distributions. They would rather tend their gardens for their own use. They do not always like to have the pigs which they have tended and cared for taken away from them and killed for the benefit of their husbands' kin group. On occasion Gururumba wives are called to the nearest coffee plantation and offered temporary jobs as coffee pickers. The men object to this employment because the women neglect their gardens and pigs during the picking and are not at all eager to share their proceeds with their husbands. This runs counter to the ideal of male dominance in making economic decisions. Children are the future strength of the group, but after a woman has had a child or two she may complain that childbearing is painful and thwart the growth of the group by refusing to have any more children. Also, women are in a position to steal semen which they can send away to sorcerers, and they are a source of contamination through menstrual blood. In a variety of ways, then, women are thought to impede activities of the lineage and sib.

The women themselves are not unaware of this attitude toward them as is evident in the following speech made to a young girl about to be sent away from her village in betrothal. The speech is part of an evening of instruction given a girl by the women of her village in the seclusion of a woman's house away from male ears:

When you get to gwota (place name) there will be many things to do. You will be told to work in the garden, to weed, to plant, to bring firewood. You must look after the pigs and bring water when you are told. You will carry heavy loads, and if they are too heavy to carry you must make two trips. You cannot ask someone else to carry part of it for you. You will give food from your garden to your husband's father and his brothers when they call out for it. When you have pigs, you will give those also, even if you have suckled them at your breast. If you do all these things people will say, "Oh, those Miruma send us good wives." If you do not, they will call you "witch" and you will be sent home before it is time to sit down with your husband (consummate the marriage).

Women are both a productive and an obstructive force in the sib. They create and withhold creation, they produce and desire to retain the fruits of production, they take semen to generate both life and death. They are like the retentive, acquisitive witch who wants but does not give.

Of Pigs and Men

The systematization of beliefs in the preceding section serves in part to illustrate an analytic technique. It compares and contrasts a number of seemingly discrete cultural items as variables along a dimension, the dimension of balance between nurturance and strength in this case. Such an arrangement is meant to emphasize those features of a set of concepts that the people who hold them see as most important for giving meaning to some situation. The analysis also prefigures a few statements concerning the Gururumba's understanding of themselves and their relationship to society. It is argued here that part of the importance these concepts have for the Gururumba is the understanding they give them of themselves.

As mentioned above, the Gururumba compare themselves to ancestors of the presocial era. One male informant said, "That is what we are really like, we are really like that, but now we understand [now that we have advanced culture]. If there were no villages or no headmen we would be like that." Other informants, independently of one another, would comment after giving an account of some ghost's unsavory behavior, "I'm like him" or "I'm like that." Informants also compared themselves with pigs that must be watched lest they eat their own offspring. On one occasion some men captured a runaway pig and were holding it over a smoking fire to calm it down since it had been on a rampage, attacking people, breaking into gardens, and ignoring entreaties to return to the fold. In an effort to explain the pig's behavior its owner said, "Pigs are like us. They tire of the rope and the fence."

These statements the Gururumba make about themselves indicate certain understandings they have of their inner nature. First, man has selfish, destructive, and aggressive impulses in himself. Witches are real people, ghosts and ancestors once were. Death releases harmful tendencies that have always been in man. Ghosts are not harmful because they are attempting to punish man or subvert his basically good nature; they are harmful in the same way men are.

Second, these impulses are curbed by the forces of society. This understanding is present in the statement that men would be like ancestors of the presocial era if they did not live in society, and in statements drawing a parallel between men and unwatched pigs. It is also implied in the notion that the display of strength is good when applied to the attainment of institutionalized goals. The Gururumba never indicated any particular longing to be like the voracious pig or the presocial ancestor, but their statements indicate an understanding that they would be that way more often than they are if it were not for social constraints. It is important to realize that in some situations they are this way. Specifically, they are this way toward other men outside the food-producing and food-exchanging group, their enemies with whom relationships are not modified by reciprocity and obligation. These are the men one can sorcerize. Killing such men is the occasion for celebration, a celebration in which even women can join by building a huge fire on a ridge top visible to the stricken group and singing derisive songs which are hopefully audible to the relatives of the deceased. These are men one can take pleasure in brutalizing when they lie wounded on the battlefield or from whom one can steal with honor. But, these are precisely the men who are outside the boundaries of society as the Gururumba know it. Within the food-exchanging group such behavior is not allowed. Sorcery does not occur here and murder is punished.

Finally, society itself represses but does not eradicate impulses that cannot be allowed expression within its boundaries. This is clearly present in the notion of harmful thoughts and in the statement that pigs, like men, ". . . tire of the rope and the fence." It is also apparent in the attitude toward men who exhibit a behavior pattern people refer to as "being a wild pig." These men run amok, attacking people and stealing objects. There is no attempt to restrain such behavior beyond keeping a watchful eye on it to avoid serious injury and no recriminations are made when it is over. The reason is that the Gururumba see such a performance as caused by certain social demands that the individual can no longer bear. The proper stance for society, then, is to withdraw and let the individual have his outlet. The name given this behavior is instructive since there are no truly wild pigs in the upper Asaro valley, only pigs that have temporarily escaped their masters.

9

Patterns and People

"There are no lightning balls."

TO THIS POINT IN the presentation the emphasis has been on pattern and form. A social morphology has been sketched out and the gross dimensions of certain concepts, beliefs, and values have been delimited. Knowing the Gururumba in this way is like knowing a region of the earth through studying a series of maps, some topographic, some climatic, and some demographic. Being in the landscape and looking at a map are two quite different experiences, however. For one thing, a map necessarily excludes some of the variety in the landscape. For another, looking at a map is not equivalent to using it. Similarly, human behavior is not fully analogous to the traveler moving through a landscape with map in hand: It is not simply a matter of following directions, for men can create new directions and new cultural landscapes. Remember, too, that one can become lost even with a map.

In this chapter our aim will be to know the Gururumba as one knows them individually and as one sees them operating within the cultural patterns I have described. Such a presentation could be systematic, but this one will present incidents and situations that have occurred in the life histories of individuals. It should be emphasized that none of the incidents described here represent deviant behavior as the Gururumba define it. The Gururumba do identify several kinds of deviant acts and persons, but these are not included here.

Gambiri

An important part of an adult man's life among the Gururumba consists of participation in exchange activities. As we have seen, one of the ways he can display himself as a fully functioning person is actively to seek out involvement in such affairs. However, not all men are as successful in these endeavors as others so that some men become leaders and others do not. Within the group who do not, there is quite a range of variation in the adaptation they make and the attitudes of others toward them. There are men who because of low intelligence or mental abnormalities barely function at all. These are deviant by Gururumba standards. There are "outside men," men who never form an allegiance of significant duration to any group they may be affiliated with and wander from one group to another. These are also deviant. Occasionally one discovers men who live out their lives in semiseclusion away from the village of their kinsmen and age mates. These are not deviants to the Gururumba because they do remain attached to a local unit, but they participate in group affairs so infrequently that they are seldom taken into account when decisions are being made.

There is another kind of person who while not a deviant, does not find the same degree of satisfaction and pleasure in exchange affairs as do the majority of men. A person like this is placed in a difficult position. He is normal in all the ways that matter to the Gururumba, and other people assume he is motivated and satisfied in the same way they are. He does not see himself in this way, however, and wants to reduce his involvement in exchange affairs without withdrawing from some participation in them or other spheres of group activity.

Several factors create frustration in such an individual. His situation can be characterized as one in which the pressures and demands of the exchange system itself are sufficient to create frustration, but not deep feelings of alienation. Gambiri was such a man. He was in his midthirties, married, had one small child, and his wife was pregnant with a second. Miruma was not Gambiri's natal village but his wife's. It is not unusual for a man to take up residence in his wife's village, in fact it is usually a move calculated to be of some advantage. In Gambiri's case, however, it eventually created a series of difficulties in his life having major consequences for his own adjustment to the dominant patterns of adult male culture.

Soon after Gambiri became married he found himself in the rather difficult economic position of all young married men in this society. His kinsmen and village mates had provided the food and wealth necessary to make the brideprice payment at his betrothal and had also supplied food at the numerous small gift exchanges occurring between affinally related groups during the betrothal period. After the couple form a domestic unit, pressure to repay this aid is put on the young man in the form of direct requests for food and wealth, and indirectly in the form of obligations to contribute to the gift exchanges of kinsmen and village mates. It should be remembered that all exchange activity relates to the acquiring of renown, and the help that a young man, or anyone else receives, may be a calculated political ploy. Failure to repay or to contribute to someone else's exchange, then, is not simply a matter of failing to meet an obligation, it is a roadblock on someone's way to renown. The pressures to repay are therefore heavy, and if a young man is not sufficiently aggressive in his pig-tending and gardening, if he is not assertive enough to make others indebted to him, or if he sustains any drastic personal misfortunes, he may find himself in a seemingly inextricable situation. Gambiri's life history indicates he was in essentially this kind of position when he decided to leave his natal village. Also, his gardens were not doing well there because of poor soil, according to Gambiri, and he felt his father-in-law's land would yield a better crop.

Economic demands and pressure to become more deeply involved in exchange activities were too great for Gambiri in his own natal village, so he left. To him it appeared a good move. However, new sets of demands were made on him in Miruma as his new village mates began attempting to draw him into their affairs, the old debts were still there, and he had cut off one possible source of aid by leaving his own kinsmen. His wife's lineage was not willing to help Gambiri discharge any obligations incurred at his marriage and, besides, they considered it somewhat of a triumph to have their daughter return after having received bride-price for her. If Gambiri had waited until some of his debts had been discharged and his wife had been longer removed from her own natal group this probably would not have been the case.

Gambiri simply did not know how nor did he really care to cope with it. He was interested in his gardens and his child, and he liked to participate in some small way in the larger-scale exchanges, but the intricacies of exchange were oppressive demands rather than interesting challenges to him. The real problem for a person like Gambiri is to convince others of this fact without appearing to be deviant or without drastic loss of social support. A relatively young man like Gambiri does not want to announce withdrawal or weakness, and other people tend to attribute his failures to unfamiliarity with economic affairs. They tend not to see him as a different kind of person but just as someone who needs a bit more time to develop.

One day Gambiri began exhibiting the behavior the Gururumba describe as "being a wild pig." For three days he roamed about the village and its environs attacking people, bursting into houses and stealing things. His actions had all the classic signs of anxiety hysteria: his speech and hearing were partially blocked, he had lost full motor and respiratory control, he behaved irrationally, and when he did speak it was either in the form of commands or blatantly false statements. The onset of this attack was sudden and when it was over, he claimed no memory of it.

There are several features of this affair to be noted. First, Gambiri's actions were not so much concerned with people as they were with objects. He stole a large net bag, and at the end of the three days it was full of things taken from others. He destroyed all this material at the end of his attack. Second, people not only did not attempt to restrain him in any way, but they felt he should be allowed to take things. To be sure, they put valuable objects out of his reach if he were known to be near, but always conspicuously left something out for him to carry away. Third, after the attack was over no mention of it was made to Gambiri nor was he made to pay compensation for any of the damage done. Fourth, Gambiri left the village for several days after the attack and while he was gone people talked about him, about his attack and its meaning, and about his past. In these conversations there was explicit recognition of the economic pressures on him and his inability to cope with them. There have been other men like Gambiri in the past and this behavior syndrome has come to have this meaning for the Gururumba. In fact, they can predict how such a man will act once an attack starts as indicated by their secreting of valuables. Finally, in the months following Gambiri's return there was an observable reduction in the intensity with which people attempted to draw him into their exchange affairs or use him as an avenue to establish exchange relationships.

Gambiri was a man who saw himself as committed to the basic patterns of Gururumba life, and as gaining some satisfactions from conforming to them, if only he could be allowed to operate at something less than the expected level of intensity in exchange affairs. Others finally came to realize this when he presented himself as others appeared to him—as demanding and taking in an aggressive manner. This realization then opened the way for him to achieve a more personally satisfying adjustment to his society.

Tomu

After young girls have passed their first menstruation, their lives take on a new and distinctive pattern. Before, they spent most of their time with their mothers performing small tasks in the garden or playing in mixed groups of other children. There were points of pleasure and excitement during this period, for small girls are frequently decorated lavishly when the men dance and accompany them onto the dance ground where they are admired by the assembled audience. There were also life-cycle rituals when they received new names, new hair arrangements, or facial tatoos that made them the center of attention. It is the period between first menstruation and betrothal that remains unique in their lives, however, in terms of the freedom of action and personal expression allowed. It will not be until they are old women that a similar freedom will again be possible.

Tomu was about sixteen or seventeen at the time of the field study. Some of her age mates had already been betrothed and had left the village. Indeed, some were betrothed before they menstruated. For some time she and several other girls had occupied an old house in the village belonging to Tomu's father. They lounged there during the day and went about largely as whim directed them. Very little is expected of such girls in the way of helping in the tasks of daily routine, although they do not withdraw completely from productive tasks. Their physical activity is reduced enough however, so they tend to put on weight, but that is not altogether undesirable, since it is thought to contribute to their handsomeness. Tomu and the other girls lavished a great deal of attention on themselves in the form of face and body painting, decorative arm bands made with the brilliant yellow fibre from orchid vines, string aprons interwoven with soft tufts of fur from forest animals, and piles of shells and beads. They seemed always to be eating and frequently slept in the daytime.

Sleeping in the daytime was not unrelated to their total pattern of activity because the abiding concern of these girls was participation in evening courting sessions. These occur when a girl invites a boy to serenade her. The boy recruits his age mates as a chorus and they proceed to the girl's house after dark. The girl has her friends present, and as the boys arrange themselves in a circle with their backs to the fire, the girls form a circle around them with their backs to the wall of the house. The boys sing long, complicated love songs in falsetto voices imitating the twittering of birds, each chorus being punctuated by a stylized sound intended to resemble a heart-rending sigh. The girls respond with songs extolling their own virtues. Various kinds of sexual play may occur during such a session as well. The girls are in control of this whole situation for they do the inviting and initiate the sexual play.

Girls who are not betrothed early may spend several years in this kind of activity. As they grow older, they spend more and more time primping and devote more and more energy to arranging serenades. It sometimes happens that these girls develop a feeling of independence and ability to control their own affairs that is not commensurate with reality. Such was the case with Tomu. She admired a boy very much and invited him many times to serenade her. He always came. She spoke to her parents about him, indicating to them she would like to marry him, but they were evasive and spoke of other possibilities. Finally, Tomu decided to take matters into her own hands. She went to the boy's village, sat down in front of the men's house, and announced to the men inside that she had come to present herself for betrothal to the young man she admired. The response of the men was graceful and even tender. They came outside, sat around Tomu, and explained the impossibility of her suggestion: No discussion of the matter had been carried on with her kinsmen, no one from her group had come to suggest a bride price, and other plans were being considered for the boy's betrothal. Tomu became quite upset and cried and beat the ground with her fists. By this time a crowd had gathered and Tomu was given over to the care of the women. They took her to a woman's house, the men began preparing an earth oven, and Tomu's parents were sent for. While food was being prepared, Tomu was calmed, and the women oiled her body and also dressed her in a new set of aprons including a special one made of bark strips rather than string. When Tomu's parents arrived they were presented with food as compensation for the embarrassment caused them, and Tomu was also fed to compensate for the rejection.

Tomu's action can be understood in cultural terms as the result of a conflict in norms. Arranging marriages is primarily a matter for adult decision in the cultural world of adults. But, in the youth culture of girls this cultural fact its only dimly realized and may be further obscured by the freedom they have in choosing their own courting partners. For girls like Tomu, the realization that they do not control the final selection of a mate may create a feeling of rebelliousness in them which manifests itself in marital instability during their early years.

Namo

Being married is the normal condition for Gururumba adults. No institutions demand celibacy, and no individuals feel remaining single would be of any particular value for them. Occasionally, very old men and women do not remarry after their mate dies, but if a person is productive at all, a new mate will be sought. For example, an old woman may marry into a polygynous family unit not as a sexual partner for the male but because she can contribute to gardening, pig-tending, and child care. No one seems occupied with how to remain single, but how to get married has perplexed some.

Arrangements for a man's first wife are made by the older males in his lineage. They carry out all the negotiations, assemble the bride price, and engineer the rituals and gift exchanges accompanying this procedure. As we have seen before, these older men are interested in widening the scope of their exchange activities or strengthening already existing ties so that the selection of a bride and the timing of betrothal is partly dependent on economic and political considerations. Ideally, the older men in a lineage begin thinking about arranging a betrothal for their unmarried sons sometime after the taboo period following initiation is over. A betrothal is arranged, the girl is brought to the village where she remains under the tutelage of her in-laws until her husband-to-be is deemed strong enough to enter the dangerous business of procreation. The husband-to-be will be in his middle or late twenties by this time. Also, ideally, all the young men who are age mates should become betrothed at about the same time.

A variety of circumstances can postpone betrothal, however, with the result that a young man finds himself in the position of being the only one of his age group who is not betrothed. This is what happened to Namo, a young man of about twenty-five. Namo's father, Bambu, was an old man who had been active in exchange affairs, but had never made a special name for himself. He only had one wife, but his marriage had been stable and he had two surviving children of whom Namo was the youngest. Namo's brother Luiso was about twenty-nine or thirty and had been married for two or three years. Namo's father's elder brother's sons were all married and had children, so that Namo was not only the only one in his age set who was not married, he was also the only eligible male in his lineage not married.

Namo had made it plain to his kinsmen that he wanted a wife, but he was told he would have to wait. The marriage of Namo's brother had severely taxed his father's resources, and Bambu and Luiso were still in the process of reciprocating the aid given in this marriage by Bambu's elder brother and his sons. Since Bambu had not been particularly energetic in exchange affairs there were few men outside his lineage willing to help in accumulating the bride price. Further, neither Bambu nor his brother had any daughters old enough to become betrothed, which cut off one possible source of wealth for the lineage. In addition to all this, Bambu's brother's eldest son was becoming quite active in exchange affairs in the context of the ward and exerted pressure on Bambu to contribute what resources he had to aid him. A betrothal would be arranged for Namo "soon," it was said, but he would have to be patient.

A promised betrothal was of little consolation to Namo. He expressed shame at being the only one of his group without a wife and anger at his kinsmen for not meeting a lineage obligation. Namo was simply caught and there was little he could do about it since he wielded no real economic or political power. Certain unusual actions Namo took can be viewed as reactions using existing cultural patterns to force a deeper realization of his plight on the members of his lineage in the hope of quicker action on his betrothal.

First, Namo had accumulated a small amount of cash by working for me as a guide. He treasured this as wealth to be used in his betrothal, keeping it locked in a wooden chest entrusted to me for safekeeping. At about the time the situation described above began to develop he took the box away. This in itself was odd because he was keeping his treasure secret to prevent its being siphoned off by lineage commitments. Shortly after this a dog belonging to someone in Namo's lineage killed a chicken belonging to a man in another lineage of the same ward. Heated words were exchanged, but as sometimes happens in a case like this, no demand for compensation was made. Without consulting anyone, Namo took his money and gave all of it, including the box it was in, to the man whose chicken had been killed. The amount of money was small, but it was far in excess of any compensation that might have been paid even if it had been demanded. His father and brother reprimanded him for doing a foolish thing, but he replied with some eloquence that he was only meeting a lineage obligation as any man should do. Such an exaggerated and uncalled for act was a calculated maneuver to impress others with their obligation to him.

Second, Namo also tried a more forceful maneuver involving a threat. Sometimes the boys of a village will congregate around the house where girls are being serenaded by youths from other villages and beat on the roof in a kind of mischievous prank. Namo organized such a prank, leading a group of boys much younger than himself, but carried it far beyond the limits of mischievousness. Instead of beating on the roof, he tore it apart, jumped into the house, scattered the hot coals of the fire about the room, and struck anyone coming under his hand in a wild display of ferocious behavior. It nearly burnt the house down and sent the serenaders scattering. He claimed the whole thing had only started out as a prank, but on arrival at the house a ghost bit him, which caused his wild behavior, and the ghost said it bit him because it did not like unmarried men. The implication of this being that the ghost might continue to bite him and cause similar disruptive behavior as long as he remained single.

Sekau

One would not describe the Gururumba as ridden with fear of witches, or accusations of witchcraft, but such accusations do occasionally occur. It is the rare individual indeed who might gain by allowing circumstances to develop that seemed clearly to lead to such an accusation. The problem is to manage other people's opinion in such a way that one's own behavior does not come to be seen as witchlike even when in fact it has been.

Sekau was an old woman, but amazingly active and strong for her advanced years. She was skinny and bent, but she still went to the gardens every day to weed, plant, and carry home net bags full of heavy sweet potatotes. Sekau was in a rather unique position among the women of Miruma because she was one of the oldest and certainly the most active of the old women, and because Miruma was her natal village. Her husband had come from Chimbu many years before to take up residence in his wife's village where he founded a lineage of some renown. Two of his sons were well on the way to becoming big men. In fact, they had even established their own men's house in the village, although it was still considered to be part of another ward and not a separate entity. Because of all these factors, Sekau exerted a great deal of influence in the village for a woman, even to having her opinion sought on matters of exchange. Consequently, she was in the habit of speaking her mind in public when affairs of the village were being discussed—a practice younger women or women of less prestige would not be able to carry off.

It happened that a dog belonging to Sekau's son died, and since dog meat is food for the Gururumba, it became the occasion for a small food distribution. Sekau's son divided the dog in such a fashion that almost all the meat went to his wife's father, the man who had given him the dog in the first place. Sekau got none of the meat, which angered her. In the midst of the food distribution, standing before the assembled guests, Sekau chastised her son for not giving her a share of the meat. She was told it was none of her business what her son did with his own dog, but she persisted in her complaints until several people were involved in trying to quiet her. No one supported her, and as tempers rose someone shouted in anger that she was acting like a witch. At that point Sekau stalked away and the situation returned to normal.

In talking with Sekau after this incident it became quite clear that the charge she was a witch worried her a great deal. It is true that accusations of this sort made in the heat of argument are not intended seriously, but Sekau realized she *had* been acting like a greedy, acquisitive witch and, furthermore, that her general position in the village might cause people to think of her in this way even more certainly. Sekau was wise enough to know that out of just such circumstances real accusations of witchcraft grow. She also knew there was no very obvious or direct course of action she could take to undo what had been done.

Several days later, while walking through some brush, a branch displaced by the person walking in front of Sekau snapped back unexpectedly hitting her in the face. It scratched her face and also made a scratch on her eyeball. It was very painful and in a few days the wound was infected to the point where her eye was swollen shut. An accident of this magnitude has supernatural causation for the Gururumba, and of all the possible causes to which it could have been attributed, Sekau chose to say it was the ghost of her husband punishing her for acting in such a nasty manner at her son's food distribution.

It will be remembered that in an earlier chapter ghosts were characterized as being unconcerned with punishment of the living for misdeeds they might have committed. This characterization emerged from asking people in what kinds of situation ghosts will attack, and from examining cases of ghostly attack.

There is less variation in the elicited accounts given of the nature of ghosts than in the case material representing the way the notion of ghost is actually used. Ghosts do have certain well-defined characteristics including capriciousness and unpredictability. Consequently within certain limits the notion of ghost can be applied to situations one would not ordinarily associate with it. A notion like ghost is meant to be used in situations, and to be useful it must have a certain flexibility. In Sekau's case, we see culture put to work: the map is used and modified to the user's need. Sekau was trying to avoid the accusation of witchcraft and the consequent punishment. Interpreting her eye injury as a ghost-caused punishment was a conscious or unconscious attempt to avoid punishment for the same fault by being "proved" a witch.

After Sekau announced the cause of her eye injury a small ritual was held to placate the ghost in order to heal the eye. It did not work, however, and Sekau became seriously ill as the infection spread through her body. The original diagnosis must have been wrong, therefore, and at this point Sekau announced she had had a dream in which a witch was revealed as the cause of the accident. By revealing this dream, Sekau made a serious accusation of witchcraft and a divination was subsequently held to discover who in the village was a witch. This second diagnosis was not unusual at all since Sekau was in a position of strength in the village and witches are prone to attack such people, but there were many other causes that she could have invoked. The fact that this cause rather than another was put forth is explicable, I feel, as a further means of dissociating herself from a possible witchcraft accusation because it made her the victim rather than the perpetrator of witchcraft.

LEnduwe

A great deal has been said about male dominance and assertiveness among the Gururumba, recognized as a desirable mode of behavior. We have also seen in the notion of harmful thoughts that this can create interpersonal hostility within the food-producing unit, with unfortunate consequences. If animosities between individuals reach a point of great intensity, open hostility may break out. In a sense, this is good because various social machineries then begin to operate to restore the relationship. If animosities remain hidden so that no drastic breach is created, this, too, can be dealt with in the ritual that assuages harmful thoughts. Another kind of situation, for which the culture offers no ready solution, is the sudden spiteful outburst that devastates another person, catches him off guard, and overwhelms him with shame. To be assertive a man must maintain self-confidence and must wield power in some form, but there are moments in a man's life when his self-confidence is undermined and power cannot be brought effectively into play.

LEnduwe was in his late thirties and had been married for several years to the same woman, but was without children. A man in this position would usually have sent his wife back to her kinsmen charging her with barrenness or would have taken a second wife. LEnduwe did neither of these things largely because of a deep personal attachment between them. Gururumba marriages are typically unstable in the early years, and although a couple may achieve a mutually satisfying adjustment after a time, it is unusual to find a man and woman with the kind of attachment that obtained between this pair. As sometimes happens with childless couples in our own culture, LEnduwe and his wife had a pet dog on which they lavished a degree of care and attention usually reserved for children. There was nothing special about the animal, it was just a scrawny, half-wild mongrel like other dogs in the village. The dog got fed a little more often than other dogs, but mostly it got petted, carried, and fondled while other dogs received little or nothing resembling affection from their masters.

One afternoon while LEnduwe was sitting with a group of people around a recently opened earth oven eating the food distributed at a naming ceremony, a woman strode into the village with a mangled chicken in her hands. She was wailing loudly so that her entrance onto the scene did not go unnoticed. She threw the bloody carcass into LEnduwe's lap and shouted, "Your child has killed my chicken," then launched into a long tirade against LEnduwe for pampering his "child" instead of training it properly. LEnduwe's dog was identified as the culprit beyond doubt as she described the animal she had seen kill her chicken, in terms that ridiculed LEnduwe's relationship to the dog.

Knowing the culture, and knowing LEnduwe to be a man in control of his position and resources, it would be predicted that such a display would have brought LEnduwe to his feet chastising the woman for making a public spectacle over such a small matter and offering compensation on the spot. He could have done this easily and done it in such a way as to make the woman look foolish. Instead he sat quite still and continued eating, responding in no visible way to the woman but concentrating all his attention on the food in front of him. His dog was sitting beside him and it appeared that LEnduwe had extended one hand toward the dog in a gesture of protection. It quickly became apparent, however, that he was attempting to choke the dog to death. Others became aware of this as the gasping and struggling of the dog increased in violence. All activity stopped as people watched with amazement. It was completely silent except for the slight sounds LEnduwe made as he ate and the noises of strangulation. Several minutes passed in stunned silence, but the dog did not die. Finally, someone took the dog away and in an awkward, bungling fashion tried to kill it by hitting it on the head with a sweet potato. People began to move once more and someone else tried a stick, but it was too small and broke. Another man stepped forward, arranged a noose, and hung the dog by the neck from a protruding house rafter which eventually brought an end to its life. Through all this LEnduwe continued to eat. The woman simply left.

LEnduwe's reaction to this situation was complex but relates primarily to his emotional involvement with the dog. No one, even jokingly, had ever referred to the dog as his "child" nor had there been any sentiment expressed to him about his childless condition. He speculated with others about possible reasons for it but nothing more. Suddenly he was confronted with the possibility that others thought him ridiculous because of this and, as he said later, "People saw my mouth," an idiom expressing great shame. For that moment he lost his ability to control the situation as it might have been controlled because he no longer knew the basis on which others responded to him. It was only when others completed the task he could not fully bring himself to do that the basis was affirmed as unchanged and interaction allowed to proceed.

DaBore

For the purposes of certain kinds of research it is convenient to think of societies like the Gururumba as relatively homogeneous. There is no class system, nor a complex division of labor, and many political and economic processes are embedded in kin and local groups. One expects to find little ideological variation in such a system, and the variation one does find is not of the same magnitude as in a structurally complex society. The difficulty with this convenience is that it does not direct our thinking to the existing variability and may thereby obscure the relationship between patterns as we describe them and human behavior as it occurs.

When lightning strikes a tree the electrical discharge sometimes appears to roll down the trunk and disappear into the ground. The Gururumba have seen this happen enough to believe that the ground near a tree struck by lightning will have a lightning ball in it somewhere. Such balls, if they can be found, are prized as objects usable in garden magic. As a result, whenever lightning strikes a tree men gather during the lightning exorcism ceremony to hunt for these balls. They dig holes, sometimes fifteen or twenty feet deep near the tree in this quest, and they frequently find things in the ground thought to be lightning balls. They are usually odd-looking pieces of decomposed stone, although badly rotted wood and bone have also been identified in this way.

I was sitting on the edge of one of these holes one day when a man named DaBore came along and sat down beside me. He asked the men in the hole what they were doing, and after they explained, he turned to me and said, "There are no lightning balls." He then got up and walked away. The men in the hole laughed at my surprise and assured me that as long as they had known DaBore he had never believed lightning balls could be found in the ground or that they were good for anything even if they could be found. As far as could be discovered, this was the only part of the supernatural belief system he did not believe in. He had no rationale for his disbelief, nor did it stem from trying one out and finding it did not work. Like other men he had a spirit house in his garden, and attributed his various illnesses and misfortunes to ghosts, sorcerers, and witches. There was nothing in his life history or his position in society that would help explain it; he just did not believe in them.

One might speculate that variation of this order, equivalent to minor variations in dress or personal taste, identify a person's individuality and function psychologically to maintain the self—other boundary. In studies of culture, the inclusion of this kind of variation seems unnecessary, but it serves us here as a reminder that people see themselves apart from the patterns of their culture and to some extent mold those patterns to their own needs. DaBore's case and the others in this section, also, serve as a reminder that knowing a cultural description of the Gururumba is knowing them in a special sense, which goes only a little way toward knowing how to be a Gururumba.

Glossary

AFFINES. Kinsmen related by marriage.

ANTHROPOMORPHISM. The ascription of humanlike attributes to nonhuman phenomena.

CLAN. A social group recruited on the basis of common descent and common residence.

CONSANGUINEALS. Kinsmen related by descent.

ENDOGAMOUS. A social group is endogamous when members of the group feel that proper marriage partners come from inside the group.

EXOGAMOUS. A social group is exogamous when members of the group feel that proper marriage partners come from outside the group.

GENEALOGY. A systematic representation of the recognized kinsmen of a person.

LINEAGE. A corporate group in which recruitment is based primarily on a rule of unilinear descent. Resident lineage is used here to mean the lineage one is residing with as opposed the natal lineage, the lineage one was born into.

PATRILINEAGE. A lineage in which membership is defined on the basis of the genealogical linkage between fathers and their children.

PATRISIB. A sib in which the constituent units are patrilineages.

PHRATRY. A group of sibs occupying contiguous territory, committed to common defense, and recognizing a common origin.

POLYGAMOUS. A marriage pattern in which a man may legitimately have more than one wife simultaneously.

SIB. A loosely structured series of kin groups among which the genealogical relationships are vaguely defined.

TEKNONOMY. The practice of addressing an individual as the parent of his or her child. Instead of addressing a man by his name, for example, he is addressed as, "Father of ———— (name of the child)."

UXORILOCAL. A mode of residence in which the household of a married pair is established in the community under the sponsorship of the wife.

VIRILOCAL. A mode of residence in which the household of a married pair is established in the community under the sponsorship of the husband.

WARD. Political divisions of a village.

Recommended Reading

AUFENANGER, HEINRICH, The Kanggi Spirit in the Central Highlands of New
   Guinea. *Anthropos* 55:671–688, 1960.
   A descriptive article concerned with the various forms of belief in de-
   moniacal nature spirits found in highlands New Guinea.
BARNES, J. A., African Models in the New Guinea Highlands. *Man* 62: 5–9,
   1962.
   A discussion of differences between African and New Guinea lineage
   systems.
BERNDT, R. M., Excess and Restraint: Social Control Among A New Guinea
   Mountain People. Chicago: The University of Chicago Press, 1962.
   An analysis of the way various aspects of culture and society impinge on
   the individual as socializing forces. Rich in case material.
BROWN, PAULA, Chimbu Tribes: Political Organization in the Eastern High-
   lands of New Guinea. *Southwestern Journal of Anthropology* 16:22–35,
   1960.
   An analysis of the organizational principles of Chimbu tribes.
LEAHY, MICHAEL AND M. CRAIN, The Land That Time Forgot: Adventures
   and Discoveries in New Guinea. New York: Funk and Wagnalls Company,
   1937.
   An autobiographical account of discovery and early exploration of the east-
   ern highlands.
LUZBETAK, L. J., The Socio-religious Significance of a New Guinea Pig Festival.
   Anthropological Quarterly 27:102–128, 1954.
   The symbolism and social function of the pig festival.
MEGGITT MERVYN, Growth and Decline of Agnatic Descent Groups Among
   the Mae Enga of the New Guinea Highlands. *Ethnology* 1:158–165, 1962.
   Important because of the insight it gives into the nature of descent groups
   in the western highlands.
NILLES, JOHN, Natives of the Bismark Mountains, New Guinea. *Oceania*
   14:104–123, 15: 1–18, 1943.
   General ethnography of peoples in the upper Chimbu valley.
READ, K. E., Nama Cult of the Central Highlands, New Guinea. *Oceania* 23:
   1–25, 1952.
   A descriptive account and analysis of the symbolism of the men's secret
   cult among the Gahuku-Gama of the lower Asaro valley.
   Cultures of the Central Highlands, New Guinea. *Southwestern Journal
   of Anthropology* 10: 1–43, 1954.
   A general survey of cultural variation in the highlands.
   Leadership and Consensus in a New Guinea Society. *American Anthro-
   pologist* 61:425–436, 1959.

A discussion of the personality type of men who rise to positions of leadership in Gahuku-Gama society.

REAY, MARIE, The Kuma: Freedom and Conformity in the New Guinea Highlands. Carlton: Melbourne University Press, 1959.

General ethnography of peoples living in the Wahgi valley.

SALISBURY, R. F., From Stone to Steel: Economic Consequences of a Technological Change in New Guinea. London and New York: Cambridge University Press, 1962.

An analysis of changes wrought in Siane society by the introduction of steel tools, money, and other elements of Western economy.

DATE DUE

Demco, Inc. 38-293